THE RED FLAG PLAYBOOK

A Tactical Guide for Passive Real Estate Investors

CARSON JONES

Copyright © 2025 by Carson Jones
ISBN: 979-8-9991448-0-5
Published by RLJ Group

All rights reserved.
No part of this publication may be reproduced, distributed, stored, or transmitted in any form or by any means—digital, physical, photocopying, recording, or otherwise—without the prior written permission of the publisher, except in the case of brief quotations used in reviews or academic work.

Disclaimer
This book reflects the personal experiences, opinions, and perspectives of the author. It is intended for informational purposes only and does not constitute financial, legal, or tax advice. Nothing in this book should be interpreted as a solicitation to buy or sell any security.

Every effort has been made to ensure the accuracy of the information provided. However, the author and publisher make no guarantees regarding the completeness, reliability, or applicability of the content. Investing—particularly in syndications—carries inherent risks, including the potential loss of capital. Not all risks or variables are discussed within this book.

Readers are strongly encouraged to consult with qualified financial, legal, and tax professionals before making any investment decisions. The strategies described may not be suitable for your individual circumstances.

The author and publisher disclaim any liability for loss or damage resulting directly or indirectly from the use or misuse of the material in this book. No warranty may be created or extended by sales materials, endorsements, or representations.

Any references to companies, products, or services are included for illustrative purposes only and do not constitute endorsements. All trademarks, product names, and brands mentioned are the property of their respective owners.

CONTENTS

Betting on Yourself Without Going It Alone vii

PART I: RED FLAGS IN HOW WE THINK ABOUT WEALTH

Chapter 1: The Illusion of Security 3
Chapter 2: When Control Becomes a Cage 11

PART II: UNDERSTANDING SYNDICATIONS

Chapter 3: How Syndications Work—and Where They Fail 23
Chapter 4: Returns and Cash Flow—What Passive Investors Should Expect 37
Chapter 5: Exit Strategies—The Most Overlooked Risk in the Deal 47

PART III: PROTECTING YOUR CAPITAL

Chapter 6: How to Screen Deals Without Getting Burned 57
Chapter 7: The Red Flags You Can't Afford to Miss in a Syndication 71
Chapter 8: When Things Go Sideways—Red Flags in the Rough . . 81
Chapter 9: Red Flags in the Rearview 91

PART IV: CAPITAL, STRATEGY, AND ASSET CLASSES

Chapter 10: Red Flags in Capital Raising 107
Chapter 11: Understanding Asset Classes—What You're Actually Investing In 113

PART V: THINKING LIKE A WEALTH BUILDER

Chapter 12: How Economic Conditions Reveal Red Flags 139
Chapter 13: From Scarcity to Strategy—Rewiring the Red
　　　　　　Flags in Your Money Mindset 149
Chapter 14: The Red Flags That Derail the Long Game 153

PART VI: 🔧 LP TOOLKIT = SUPERPOWER SECTION

Chapter 15: The Red Flag Deal Review Checklist 159
Chapter 16: Spot the Jockey—Before You Bet the Farm 167
Chapter 17: Ask Like Your Wealth Depends on It. 173
Chapter 18: How AI Is Reshaping Real Estate—And
　　　　　　Revealing Red Flags in Plain Sight 181
Chapter 19: Where to Start. 187

PART VII: BONUS TAX TRAPS AND STRATEGIC ADVANTAGES

Chapter 20: Tax Strategy for LPs—Depreciation, K-1s, and
　　　　　　Red Flags 197
Chapter 21: 1031 Exchanges, Self-Directed IRAs &
　　　　　　Opportunity Zones 211
Chapter 22: Tax Pitfalls—What CPAs Wish LPs Knew. 227

PART VIII: THE BIGGER PICTURE

The Reason We Do It All. 239
Glossary & Calculations 245

Want more resources or to be added to our email list scan the QR code below.

https://go.passive.investments/info

Having trouble with the QR code?
Feel free to email us directly at **carson@passive.investments**
(Note: There's no ".com"—".investments" is the full domain.)

INTRODUCTION
BETTING ON YOURSELF WITHOUT GOING IT ALONE

This book is about cutting through the noise.
It's a tactical guide to help you avoid the most common traps that take down smart investors—not because they're reckless, but because they never learned what to look for.

You'll learn how I moved from chasing paychecks to allocating capital—and the hard lessons that shaped how I evaluate deals today. We'll break down how syndications work, where the landmines are, and how to spot red flags most investors miss. Because the real risks—and rewards—aren't just in the numbers, but in the assumptions, the structure, the operator, and your own thinking.

You won't just learn to spot red flags from the outside looking in. We'll also walk you through the mental traps that even seasoned business owners and high-earning professionals fall into—often without realizing it—using hard-won lessons from my own experience. And we'll pull back the curtain on what really happens once you're inside the deal: the red flags that only reveal themselves under contract, on-site, or buried deep in the numbers.

From a **due diligence standpoint**, these are warning signs we've personally encountered:

- Inability to produce financials in a reasonable timeframe
- Financials cobbled together in Excel with no real accounting system
- Multiple expired leases or leases that don't match the rent roll

- Collections that look solid—until you realize they're choppy and unreliable

From a **physical standpoint**, the signs are more subtle—but just as revealing:

- A parking lot full of cars at 10am (who's actually working?)
- "Occupied" units with no belongings, no signs of life, and no real tenant

We'll walk through how to spot the warning signs, what they actually mean, and how to protect your capital before the wire ever goes out.

What should you really look for in a sponsor?

It's easy to assume that background checks and legal history are the most important pieces of the puzzle, but that's only part of the picture.

Take SEC violations, for example; most are civil, not criminal. Many won't even show up on a standard background check.

Bankruptcies? In commercial real estate, most loans are non-recourse. That means sponsors rarely file for bankruptcy—they just hand the keys back to the bank. But not before making a cash call to investors, trying to salvage the deal on someone else's dime.

How important is skin in the game?

It's one of the first questions investors ask:

"How much skin does the sponsor have in the deal?"

And it's a fair question. You want aligned interests—and we'll break that down in this book.

But here's the nuance most people miss:

In today's environment, almost every deal requires some form of capital. That might be hard cash, earnest money, due diligence deposits, or other upfront risk.

That said, I'm impressed when a sponsor can negotiate terms so strong—through seller financing, creative structuring, or a deeply discounted price—that the bank doesn't require traditional money down.

It's not just about how much money the sponsor puts in. It's about how they behave when things *don't* go according to plan.

Skin in the game is important.
But character in the fire? That's what really protects your capital.

▶ **Skin in the game can be misleading.**

Even when a sponsor claims to have money in the deal, a dishonest operator can quietly siphon it back out—through acquisition fees, inflated operating expenses, or stacked "management" charges.

Just because they say they've invested doesn't mean the money's still in the deal.

So always follow the incentives.
Look at *how* the sponsor is getting paid—and *when*.

True alignment isn't just about an upfront check.
It's about whether the sponsor wins *with* you… or *regardless* of you.

The better question is how are our interest aligned? Skin in the game is only part of that.

A Sponsor Should Be Able to Clearly State Their Edge.
If they can't explain their advantage in 30 seconds, they probably don't have one.

Here's mine:
We buy at a low basis.
That means less downside risk, stronger cash flow, and more resilient equity—without gambling on appreciation. We source off-market, stabilized deals through trusted family office networks, not public platforms or crowdfunding sites.

This isn't just another investing book.
The Red Flag Playbook is packed with practical insights—from real-world horror stories to tactical tools—and it doesn't let up. With a can't-miss **Chapter 18 on how Artificial Intelligence is reshaping real estate diligence**, and a detailed **Glossary that breaks down the elusive waterfall payout structure**, this book arms passive investors with what they actually need: clarity, confidence, and red flag radar.

Who This Book Is For

This book is for the high-performing professional who's built income—but not yet true wealth.

It's for the business owner who's created something meaningful—but still feels like they're stuck in the machine.

It's for the aspiring investor who's seen syndications mentioned in passing—but doesn't fully understand how they work, what to ask, or who to trust.

Whether you've already invested in commercial real estate or are just starting to explore passive income beyond stocks, this book will help you ask sharper questions, avoid costly mistakes, and invest with confidence.

A Bit About Me

I grew up in Arlington, Texas—just across from the old Texas Rangers ballpark. If you've ever been to a summer game there, you know the feeling: heat, grit, fireworks overhead.

That same energy shaped me.

Arlington isn't Dallas or Fort Worth.
It's a working class town.
A place where nothing is handed to you—and everything is earned.

From there, I went to Baylor University, earned a BBA in Finance, and landed in corporate America. For 3.5 years, I worked in accounting and IT. It was safe. Predictable. Comfortable.

But that comfort came with a ceiling.
And I was never built to climb someone else's ladder.

So I started building my own.

I ran restaurant franchises. Started a marketing agency. Learned through wins and losses what it takes to create something from scratch. Over time, I moved from entrepreneur to investor—ultimately becoming a Fund Manager and Real Estate Syndicator.

Today, I manage investor capital, structure deals, and identify opportunities that others overlook. I now live in the Nashville, TN area—where I continue to build relationships, raise capital, and help investors grow their wealth through smart, strategic partnerships.

But the path here was anything but straight.

Why Now?

As we enter 2025, the signals are flashing.

- Gas prices are falling.
- GDP is contracting.
- Over **$1.2 trillion** in commercial real estate debt is coming due.
- Distress is mounting—and opportunities are hiding in plain sight.

The headlines are focused on inflation and tariffs.
But the real risk?
Missing the window to capitalize on a generational wealth transfer.

This isn't just about navigating today's market.
It's about giving you the tools to vet deals in *any* market.
Bull or bear. Boom or bust.

If you're ready to move beyond hustle, control, and short-term plays…
If you're ready to build wealth that outlasts cycles…
If you want to learn how to bet smart, spot red flags, and invest with confidence…

Then let's get started.

PART I
RED FLAGS IN HOW WE THINK ABOUT WEALTH

The moment you realize this game isn't what it seems.

CHAPTER 1
THE ILLUSION OF SECURITY

Why I Left Corporate—and How That Decision Shaped My Investing Philosophy

When I first stepped into corporate America, I expected teamwork. I thought it would feel like the restaurant world—everyone hustling through the chaos together, covering for each other, sharing the win.

What I walked into instead was a masterclass in self-preservation.
Office politics.
Posturing.
Promotions based on optics, not output.

The system rewarded those who played the game—not those who improved it.
Value didn't matter as much as visibility.
And over time, that realization hit hard:
This wasn't a career.
It was a cage.

A machine that fed on your time—and gave you just enough in return to keep you quiet.
It looked stable on the outside, but it was fragile at the core.

The Breaking Point

I remember the moment I hit the wall.
"I don't care if I fail. I'm never coming back."

That wasn't just a dramatic exit line.
It was a vow—to stop trading time for a paycheck someone else controlled.

So I jumped.
First, I launched a marketing agency helping investment firms raise capital.
Then I co-ran restaurant franchises with my dad.

The work was unpredictable, messy, unstructured, but it was mine.
And it gave me something corporate life never could:
Real-world judgment.

Lessons from the Field

In entrepreneurship, there's nowhere to hide.
You learn quickly how to:

- Vet partners—and walk away from the wrong ones
- Manage cash flow when the pressure is on
- Lead through chaos—not behind policies
- Trust your gut when something doesn't feel right

What I didn't realize at the time was that these were the same skills I'd later use to evaluate investments.

As the agency grew, I started putting capital to work.
First in stocks and options. Then in private deals—real estate, energy, funds.
And as I gained experience, I built a mental model that I still use today:

The 3 Principles That Guide Every Investment I Make

1. **A Track Record of Growing Earnings**
   Hype doesn't build wealth. I want compounding performance.
2. **Strong Founders or Brands**
   I don't invest in promises—I invest in people.
3. **Scalable Growth with Staying Power**
   I want assets that last through cycles—not ones that vanish when the tide turns.

These principles started in the markets, but they've carried over into every private investment I've done since. They're also why I believe real estate—when done right—is a WE game.

The Comfort of the Familiar

Most people think they're playing it safe.
They work hard, save diligently, and hope the market cooperates.
They follow the playbook: get a job, max out the 401(k), pay off the house, and maybe—just maybe—retire by 65.

But here's the red flag: what feels safe often isn't.

The financial system is set up to make you feel like you're doing the right thing while quietly siphoning control, flexibility, and upside from your life.

Traditional retirement accounts have a place—but they come with limitations:

- You can't access the money without penalty until age 59½
- Your investment options are narrow and often fee-heavy
- Your returns are tied to markets you can't control

In truth, Wall Street wants your money on autopilot—and your eyes off the fees.

That's not security. That's sedation.

▶ Red Flag: Mistaking Delay for Discipline

There's a difference between patience and procrastination.
Too many investors "set it and forget it" in vehicles that don't align with their goals, timeline, or risk profile.

The False Promise of Diversification

You've heard it a thousand times: "Don't put all your eggs in one basket."

But here's what they don't say: spreading your money across dozens of underperforming vehicles isn't diversification—it's dilution.

Real diversification comes from:

- Asset classes with uncorrelated risk
- Tax treatment that protects your upside
- Cash flow that works in any cycle

A True Story: When Security Backfires

A friend of mine, we'll call him Matt, worked in tech and did everything "right."
401(k)? Maxed out.
Mutual funds? Check.
Company stock? All in.

Then the market turned. Tech stocks dropped.
His company froze bonuses and laid off 20% of staff.

He wasn't just hurt by the market—he was double-exposed. And the worst part?
He couldn't access most of his wealth without penalties or losses.

Security isn't about safety. It's about resilience.

The ME Game vs. the WE Game

In corporate America, and in too many businesses, people play the ME game.
They protect turf.
Chase titles.
Avoid accountability.
Scapegoat when things go wrong.

Real estate doesn't reward that long-term.
This business is different.
You win by aligning incentives, choosing the right people, and building systems that don't revolve around any one individual.

Syndications are one of the few places where this plays out clearly:

- Sponsors run the deal
- Passive investors bring the capital
- Everyone shares in the upside

But only if the right people are in place.

Too many investors treat this like a solo mission, by trying to do everything themselves.
They stay quiet instead of asking the hard questions—afraid to look inexperienced.

But real success comes from knowing when to lead—and when to lean on someone more experienced.

Red Flag Radar: The Power of Who You Know

Surrounding yourself with the right people is one of the most underrated forms of risk management.

In real estate, relationships don't just open doors—they help you avoid the wrong ones.

I recently asked my friend **Dan Lewkowicz**, who brings over 15 years of commercial real estate experience, what red flags he looks for when underwriting a deal. His answer wasn't just about numbers. It was about awareness. Pattern recognition. The kind of wisdom that comes from seeing hundreds of deals play out over time.

One of the smartest things a sponsor can do is **partner with brokers who know the terrain—and who use the tools to navigate it.**

Dan doesn't rely solely on gut instinct. He blends traditional underwriting and extensive industry experience with next-generation platforms like **Placer.AI**, using geolocation and consumer behavior data to confirm—or challenge—market assumptions before a deal ever hits his client's inbox.

We'll dive deeper into these AI tools in **Chapter 18**, but the lesson is timeless:

When you surround yourself with the right people and the right tools, you don't just find better deals—you avoid the bad ones altogether.

🔍 Expert Insight: Dan Lewkowicz on Red Flags You Can't Afford to Miss

Dan has seen deals succeed—and implode—based on details many investors overlook. Here are six red flags he watches for every time:

1. **Overly Optimistic Proformas**
   If the numbers only work in Excel, they won't work in real life. Dan scrutinizes revenue growth and expense assumptions, sales figures and other metrics line by line. If the numbers are projected, he ignores them and instead focus on real numbers and not proformas.
2. **Declining Population**
   You can't out-smart a shrinking market. Fewer people means fewer customers for your tenants—and weaker fundamentals overall.
3. **Poor Ingress/Egress**
   If tenants or customers can't get in and out easily, expect leasing headaches and long-term turnover.
4. **Poor Visibility**
   Especially in retail and mixed-use, visibility drives revenue. If you have to look hard for the building, your tenants and their customers will too.
5. **Above-Market Rent**
   If your tenant is paying rent that exceeds market comps by a wide margin, it's not a value-add—it's a value fantasy.
6. **High Market Vacancy**
   If the surrounding area is 20%+ vacant, there's a reason. Don't assume you'll be the exception.

"Proper underwriting is protection against poor asset performance."
– Dan Lewkowicz

CHAPTER 2
WHEN CONTROL BECOMES A CAGE

Escaping the Operator Trap and the Earn-and-Burn Loop

One of the most common traps I see high-income earners fall into—especially business owners and high achievers—is this:

They confuse ownership with freedom.

They believe they've graduated financially because they *own* something:

A business.
A brand.
A team.
A title.

But if your income still depends on your time, your energy, or your daily decision-making—
You didn't buy freedom.
You bought a new job—with better branding.

▶ Red Flag: When the Business Owns You

It's everywhere.

- A doctor opens a med spa.
- A tech exec buys a franchise.
- An investor grabs a restaurant and says, "This will run itself."

Spoiler: it never runs itself.

I've done it too.

I co-owned a franchise where my so-called freedom depended on whether a teenager showed up for their shift.

From the outside, it looked like success.
From the inside, it felt like stress.

Staffing issues. Payroll crunches. Tax deadlines.
It wasn't entrepreneurship—it was adult babysitting with financial liability.

The red flag isn't the business.
It's the assumption that a business needing your constant presence can somehow scale without you.

If the machine stops when you leave the room, you don't have leverage.
You have liability dressed up in LLC paperwork.

Me learning the fryer in 2009, when I thought owning the business meant freedom.

The Entrepreneurship Mirage

The hustle culture on social media sells a seductive lie:

Quit your job.
Start a business.
Build a personal brand.
Work from your laptop in Bali.

It's a lifestyle—sold by influencers, not investors.

They flaunt rented Lamborghinis, fake screenshots, and "$100K/month" claims...
But here's what they don't show you:

- The credit card debt they racked up before going viral
- The three failed businesses before the fourth went anywhere

- The endless customer support, churn, chargebacks, and chaos
- That most of their money comes from selling the dream—not running a real operation

They're not selling ownership.
They're selling *identity*—the illusion of control and status without the substance.

▶ Red Flag: When a Single-Family Rental Becomes a Second Job

It's not just businesses. I've seen plenty of investors buy "passive" rentals and end up working overtime for less than minimum wage.

One vacant unit can wipe out your monthly profit.
One bad tenant can blow up a year's return.
And one missed contractor deadline can cost you thousands.

I've got friends who've done well with single-family real estate. But I've got just as many who say: "I bought a rental—and now I own a part-time job I can't quit."

Between turnover, maintenance, property taxes, and late-night repair calls, the idea becomes a bit overwhelming.

Single-family investing *can* work.
Just make sure you're not buying passive income that turns into active stress.

The Control Fallacy

Here's the uncomfortable truth about high achievers:

We don't hate work. We hate *powerlessness*.

We love being in control.
We know every number on the P&L.

We solve every problem ourselves.
We make every final decision.

But that obsession with control becomes a cage.

We confuse presence with power.
Activity with achievement.
Hustle with ownership.

We upgrade our tools.
We upgrade our team.
We upgrade our office.

But we don't upgrade our mindset.
We're still the bottleneck. We just look better doing it.

The Moment It Clicked

My shift didn't come from a windfall.
It came from burnout.

I looked at my calendar and realized I was scheduled into every outcome.
Every decision. Every fire. Every client. Every crisis.

And when I tried to step away, things slowed—or fell apart entirely.

That's not scale. That's fragility.
That's a business built on personality, not systems.

So I changed the question.

From: "How can I earn more next quarter?"
To: "How can I own income that doesn't require me?"

That question changed everything.

From Sweat Equity to Scalable Equity

Once I stopped chasing control, I started chasing leverage.

I moved capital away from:

- Businesses that needed me daily
- Deals I had to manage personally
- People I had to train, lead, or replace

And I shifted toward investments that ran without me.

That meant learning to:

- Vet sponsors instead of employees
- Read offering memorandums instead of P&Ls
- Evaluate risk and return, not drama and deadlines

The first time I invested in a stabilized, cash-flowing real estate syndication, I realized something powerful:

The income came.
The stress didn't.

And for the first time in years, I wasn't the engine.

The Operator Trap

Even in real estate, it's easy to slide right back into "operator mode."

You start out investing...
Then next thing you know, you're:

- Managing tenants
- Monitoring rates
- Running CapEx budgets

- Calling contractors
- Arguing over invoices

Even with third-party management, the buck still stops with you.

You haven't created freedom—you've just swapped stress categories.

I know, because I tried it.
I once bought into a small apartment deal and tried to be everything:
Raise capital.
Run the rehab.
Negotiate debt.
Handle investors.

I didn't sleep for six months.

And the kicker? My returns were mediocre.

The moment I backed out and invested with a sponsor who knew the asset class better than I did, my income improved—and my anxiety disappeared.

▶ Red Flag: Confusing Involvement with Insight

There's a belief among operators that being "in the weeds" gives you an edge.

Sometimes, it just gives you tunnel vision.

The best decisions I've made didn't come from doing *more*.
They came from seeing *clearer*—because I had space.

True investing is about leverage.
Not just capital leverage—but mental leverage.

The less noise, the better your decisions.

How Founders Think Differently

Great founders—whether in business or real estate—don't build empires by doing everything themselves.

They build by creating systems that don't need them every day.

They don't obsess over control.
They obsess over alignment.

They ask:

- "Is this operator's vision aligned with mine?"
- "Do I understand their incentive structure?"
- "Does my capital grow even if I'm not in the room?"

They trade ego for efficiency.
Control for clarity.
Effort for scale.

They're not checking out—they're choosing wisely what to check in *on*.

▶ Red Flag: Mistaking Hustle for Leverage

Many investors resist passive deals because it feels too "hands off."

But that's exactly the point.

Passive income is what gives your active effort *meaning*.

It's what turns effort into equity.
Risk into reward.
Time into ownership.

You don't need to find the deal.
You don't need to be the landlord.

You don't need to manage anything.

You just need to vet the people who do.

That's what syndications offered me:

- True ownership without the day-to-day headaches
- Professional teams operating institutional-grade properties
- Cash flow, tax benefits, and scale—without the burnout

I still make decisions.
But now I make fewer—and they're worth more.

Bonus Framework: Control vs. Leverage—5 Questions to Ask Yourself

If you're stuck in the earn-and-burn loop, ask:

1. If I walked away for 30 days, would the income stop?
2. Am I solving the same problems I was solving 12 months ago?
3. Do I own systems—or do I just manage people?
4. Is my net worth growing without my effort—or only with it?
5. Is my capital working harder than I am?

If the answer to most of those is *no*, you're not an investor yet. You're still an operator.

What Real Ownership Looks Like

You've already beaten the odds.
You've built something. You've earned. You've led.

But don't let that become the ceiling.

The need to control everything is the silent killer of wealth.

Real ownership doesn't mean doing more.
It means building something that works—especially when you're not in the room.

You don't have to retire.
You don't have to disappear.

But at some point, you have to graduate—from operator to investor.

Because the real win isn't just making money.
It's getting paid without showing up.
It's keeping more through smart tax planning.
It's building a life designed to scale—not to survive.

PART II
UNDERSTANDING SYNDICATIONS

CHAPTER 3

HOW SYNDICATIONS WORK— AND WHERE THEY FAIL

When most people think about real estate investing, they picture a grind: broken toilets, late rent, and 3 AM emergency calls. It keeps a lot of smart investors stuck in what feels safer—stocks, 401(k)s, maybe a rental or two.

But here's what the wealthy have known for decades: You don't have to be a landlord to build wealth through real estate. You just need to own the right slice of the right deal—with the right people.

That's where syndications come in.

What Is a Syndication?

A syndication is a professional real estate partnership. It's like teaming up with a builder, operator, lender, and accountant—all rolled into one—and letting them do the heavy lifting while you fund the blueprint.

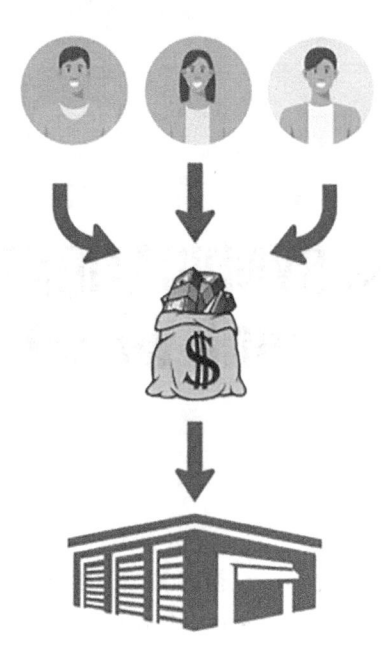

Investors pool capital, and a sponsor (or GP, General Partner) handles the entire process:

- Sourcing the property
- Securing financing
- Managing operations
- Handling reporting and investor updates
- Overseeing the exit

You provide capital. They run the deal. Everyone shares in the upside.

This model offers powerful leverage: you tap into the sponsor's time, team, experience, and pipeline—without taking on daily responsibilities yourself.

But syndications aren't magic. They only work if the structure, sponsor, and strategy are sound.

What Syndications Are NOT

Understanding what a syndication *is not* is just as important as knowing what it is:

- ✘ **Not a REIT**: You're not buying a share in a large, publicly traded fund. You're investing in a specific private deal or private fund.
- ✘ **Not a stock**: You can't click "sell" when you get cold feet. Your capital is tied up for years.
- ✘ **Not a savings account**: These investments aren't liquid, and they do carry risk.
- ✘ **Not truly passive if you skip due diligence**: You're trusting someone with your money. Trust should be earned—and verified.

Too many LPs think it's "set it and forget it." That's how good money goes bad.

Why Passive Commercial Real Estate Works

Commercial real estate (CRE) assets—like apartments, self-storage, retail centers, and industrial buildings—are valued based on net operating income (NOI), not emotional market comps. That makes CRE:

- More predictable
- Less speculative
- Easier to model and improve

When paired with the right sponsor, these assets deliver:

1. **Cash Flow** – Lease-driven income, paid monthly or quarterly.
2. **Appreciation** – "Forced appreciation" by raising rents, lowering expenses, or both.
3. **Tax Benefits** – Depreciation, bonus depreciation, and cost segregation that can offset your taxable income.

You're not buying a dream. You're buying a business.

What Makes Syndications Risky?

It's not the asset type. It's the people and the structure.

Deals fail for four main reasons:

1. Overpromising – Inflated pro formas and unrealistic assumptions.
2. Poor Management – Weak systems, poor tenant screening, or no plan for CapEx.
3. Fee Gouging – Sponsors who get paid no matter what—even if you don't.
4. Bad Timing – Acquiring the right asset at the wrong part of the cycle.

⚑ Red Flag: Confusing Delegation with Abdication
Passive doesn't mean blind. If you don't understand the capital stack, the deal's downside scenarios, or the operator's incentive structure, you're not investing—you're gambling.

Before I invest, I ask:

- How does the sponsor make money?
- What happens if cash flow stops?
- Are they using third-party management or doing it all themselves?

If they dodge or deflect—I walk.

The Syndication Lifecycle: 6 Key Phases

1. **Find the Deal**
   The sponsor identifies a property, runs underwriting, and negotiates terms. If their assumptions are off here, the whole thing falls apart.
2. **Structure It**
   The deal is placed in a legal entity (usually an LLC or LP), with clear equity splits, management roles, fees, and waterfall structure. This is where alignment is either built or broken.
3. **Raise Capital**
   Investors review the Private Placement Memorandum (PPM), subscribe, and wire funds. Read the documents. Don't rely on the webinar.
4. **Acquire & Operate**
   The sponsor closes the deal, takes over operations, and executes the business plan—often including renovations, leasing, or repositioning.
5. **Distribute Returns**
   Investors (LPs) receive periodic distributions and updates. If communication drops, that's your first warning.
6. **Exit**
   Through sale, refinance, or recapitalization. This is where the sponsor's execution either proves out—or gets exposed.

SYNDICATION LIFECYCLE

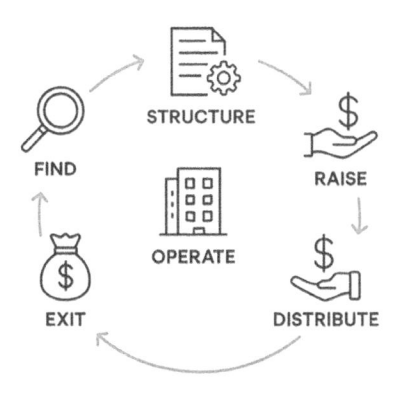

FIND → STRUCTURE → RAISE → DISTRIBUTE → EXIT → OPERATE

Each step carries its own risks. The best sponsors plan for each one and communicate clearly.

Who's Who in a Syndication

- **General Partner (GP)**: The operator in charge of execution.
- **Limited Partners (LPs)**: Passive investors who share in the upside.
- **Property Manager**: Handles tenants, maintenance, and rent collection.
- **Legal and Accounting**: Keeps the deal compliant and tax-efficient.

▶ **Red Flag: Favor Factory**

When friends and family are running key functions—especially property management—ask if there's real oversight. If the answer is "trust me," walk away.

Direct Ownership vs. Syndication

Feature	Direct Ownership	Syndication (LP)
Time Commitment	High	Low
Involvement	Active	Passive
Liability	Often Personal	Limited to Investment
Diversification	Harder	Easier
Scalability	Slower	Faster

Sample Syndication Deal Structure

Let's say a deal offers:

- **Preferred Return (Pref)**: 8%
- **Equity Split**: 70% LP / 30% GP
- **Promote**: Sponsor gets a larger share of profits after the preferred return is met

So the "waterfall" looks like:

1. First 8% to LPs
2. Catch-up to GP
3. Remaining split 70/30

Always ask:

- Does the GP make money before you do?
- Are there acquisition, asset management, refinance, or disposition fees?
- Are the preferred returns cumulative?

Deal Types: Know What You're Signing Up For

- **Single-Asset Syndication** – Clear and focused but higher concentration risk.
- **Multi-Asset Fund** – More diversification but murkier reporting and slower distributions.
- **Single-Asset Fund** – Like a hybrid: more flexibility, but you still need to vet the GP.

Real-World Examples: One Wins, One Wrecks

The Good:

- Sponsor bought a 100-unit apartment building in a growing Texas city.
- Conservative underwriting with verified rent comps.
- Used third-party management with robust reporting.
- Hit 9% preferred return year one, 15% IRR by exit in year three.

The Bad:

- Sponsor promised 20% IRR but bought at the peak.
- Deferred maintenance destroyed the budget.

- No communication for months.
- Refinanced early to return capital—but wiped out 40% of future equity in the process.

Slick marketing won't fix a shaky plan.

The Psychology of the Passive Investor

One of the biggest risks in syndication isn't the deal—it's the investor's behavior.

We fall in love with numbers.
We get excited by glossy pitch decks.
We skip the boring stuff because the sponsor "seems trustworthy."

▶ **Red Flag: "I Like Them" Is Not Due Diligence**
You're not dating the sponsor. You're investing with them.
Emotion clouds judgment. So does urgency. If they say "this deal is closing fast"—pause. Speed is a tactic. Scarcity is a tool.
Great deals are worth understanding. Bad ones are gone tomorrow.

The "Set It and Forget It" Myth

Many LPs confuse "passive" with "carefree." But here's what they miss:

- Passive means you're not operating the deal
- It does **not** mean you skip diligence
- It does **not** mean you don't ask questions
- It does **not** mean your capital is safe just because it's legal

If you wouldn't wire $100K to a stranger on Instagram, why do it for someone you barely know running an apartment deal?

Almost every syndication involves some degree of construction whether it be a minor value add or ground up development. You don't need to know everything, but you do need to know what questions to ask.

Red Flags to Watch: Choosing a Commercial General Contractor and Development Partner

Whether you're investing in ground-up construction or a heavy value-add repositioning, your success is tied to one critical player: **the developer**. Unlike stabilized assets—where the operator manages tenants and cash flow—a development project starts with dirt and a dream. That means more moving parts... and more opportunities for things to go wrong.

There are a lot of reasons I like development deals. First off, you don't get caught in bidding wars over existing assets.

Let's be real: there's almost no such thing as an "off-market" deal. There's just who gets the call first. And those calls usually start with mega-funds. That's what "access" really means—unless you create your own.

While the mega-funds compete over properties, smart family offices play a different game.

They don't chase.
They **build** on land they've been holding for years or bought at the right price.

And when they build, they call someone like **Nick Johnson**—an experienced developer and construction expert in the Nashville area with a track record of execution. He can handle projects of any size or complexity. And if it's something that's never been built before? He can handle that too or point you in the right direction with the many connections he has.

What Does a Developer Actually Do?

A developer is responsible for:

- Site selection and acquisition
- Entitlement and permitting
- Managing architects and engineers
- Overseeing construction timelines and budgets
- Coordinating financing and eventual stabilization

▶ **Red Flags When Evaluating Developers**

1. No track record in the asset class or market
A developer with multifamily experience may not be the right fit for a cold storage build. Track record in the *specific product type and location* matters more than total square footage completed.

2. Lack of in-house construction or deep GC relationships
If they're hiring the cheapest general contractor and crossing their fingers, that's not risk management—that's roulette.

3. Unrealistic timeline or budget projections
Promising a 12-month build when comps take 18 is a major flag. Compare to real-world data. If it looks too good to be true...

4. Financing not fully secured
Is the construction loan truly committed? Do they have bridge equity or gap funding lined up? Many projects die on the altar of "almost funded."

5. Permits and entitlements "in progress"
"Permitting expected soon" can stretch for months—or years. If the project relies on zoning changes or city council votes, you're betting on politics, not real estate.

6. Light on pre-development work
No soil studies? No environmental testing? No floodplain analysis? They're winging it. And you're footing the bill when surprises hit.

7. Developer wears too many hats
If they're also the broker, GC, or architect, that's a potential conflict of interest. Specialization creates accountability. Jack-of-all-trades often means master of none.

8. History of mechanic's liens or litigation
Check public records. Have they been sued by subs? Are there outstanding liens? A messy legal history is a giant red flag.

9. No contingency budget
Pro developers build in 10–20% for overruns. Amateurs act like the budget is sacred. Spoiler: it never is.

☑ **Better Questions to Ask**

- How many ground-up projects have you completed in the last 5 years?
- What went wrong on the last one—and what did you learn?
- Are your construction partners locked in with contracts?
- How are contingencies handled in your budget and financing?
- What third-party oversight do you use (e.g. owner's reps, cost consultants)?
- Can we see timelines, budgets, and lender correspondence from a prior project?

For a deeper dive on evaluating developers and construction partners, check out Nick Johnson's expert insights at the end of Chapter 11.

Nick has helped execute dozens of successful projects across retail, QSR, and build-to-suit developments. If you're considering a development-heavy deal or want a second opinion on a construction budget, he's a great person to know.

You can reach him directly at:
Nick.xj.johnson@gmail.com
615.332.2369

Why I Doubled Down on Syndications

I didn't want a second job. I wanted to build wealth while building freedom. Syndications helped me:

- Diversify without spreading myself thin
- Access larger, more stable assets I couldn't afford solo
- Reduce my tax bill through legal, strategic deductions
- Free up time to think big—and live well

But syndications taught me something else:

▶ Red Flag: Betting on Deals Instead of People

Deals are easy to dress up. But execution is hard to fake. That's why I now spend as much time vetting the sponsor as I do reviewing the numbers.

Ask yourself:

- Have they ever lost investor capital?
- What did they learn when a deal went sideways?
- Do they answer tough questions—or pivot and pitch?

Red Flags Recap—Chapter 3

1. **Confusing Delegation with Abdication** – Passive doesn't mean ignorant.
2. **No Defined Roles or Oversight** – Especially with family or friends on the team.

3. **Unrealistic Assumptions** – If it only works in Excel, it won't work in real life.
4. **Ignoring Incentives** – Know exactly how and when the sponsor gets paid.
5. **Betting on the Deal, Not the People** – Execution matters more than projections.

Final Word

Syndications offer one of the clearest paths to scalable, passive wealth. But they only work if you:

- Vet the sponsor like they're applying for a job at your company
- Understand the structure like your money depends on it—because it does
- Ask the hard questions and demand the right answers

Do that, and syndications won't just protect your capital—they'll multiply it.

Coming up next: How returns actually work—and the assumptions that make or break them.

Family Office Event I attended in Miami, where LPs and GPs came together to discuss market cycles, capital structure, and risk.

CHAPTER 4
RETURNS AND CASH FLOW— WHAT PASSIVE INVESTORS SHOULD EXPECT

Let's talk about the part everyone cares about most: getting paid.

Cash flow. Appreciation. Equity multiples. IRR.

It's easy to get seduced by the numbers. But smart investors know: the bigger the promise, the closer you should look.

In this chapter, we'll break down how returns really work—and where red flags often hide in plain sight. Because in syndications, you're not just evaluating a property. You're evaluating a payout structure. A set of assumptions. A forecast of the future.

And future-focused math has a way of sounding great... until it doesn't.

1. Distributions: When Do You Get Paid?

Most syndications offer monthly or quarterly distributions—paid via ACH straight to your bank account. It feels good. Tangible. Real.

But where's that money coming from?

Usually, it's from net operating income (NOI): what's left after rent comes in and expenses go out. But not all properties are stabilized from Day 1. Some need heavy renovation, lease-ups, or operational overhauls.

▶ Red Flag: Day 1 Distributions on a Heavy Value-Add

If a sponsor promises immediate distributions on a property that's 50% vacant and needs major rehab, ask: How is that possible?

Often, sponsors fund early distributions out of reserves or investor capital itself, creating the illusion of cash flow. But it's not real income—it's a shell game.

In a healthy deal, distributions follow NOI—not precede it.

2. Where Returns Actually Come From

There are three core drivers of returns in a typical real estate syndication:

- **Cash Flow**
  Rental income minus expenses, distributed during the hold period. This is your income stream—and often a sign of stability.
- **Bonus Income Streams**
  Parking, storage, pet fees, laundry, vending, and RUBS (Ratio Utility Billing System) can all boost NOI. These are operational levers smart sponsors pull to improve returns without raising rents.
- **Appreciation**
  When NOI grows—or when market cap rates compress—the value of the property increases. Most appreciation comes at exit, especially in value-add deals.

▶ **Red Flag: Over-Underwritten Value**
Watch for:

- Rent growth assumptions that exceed historical trends
- Operating expense budgets that seem suspiciously low
- Exit cap rates lower than entry, without clear reasoning

▶ **Red Flag: Unrealistic Rent Projections**
If projected rents are 25-30% above current market rates without comparable properties, you're looking at hope—not underwriting. Always ask:

- What's the current rent?
- What are comps renting for?
- How much CapEx is budgeted to justify those increases?

3. Preferred Returns and Profit Splits

This is where alignment either gets built—or breaks.

- **Preferred Return**
  This is the return you're promised before the sponsor participates in profits. It's typically 6-8%, and meant to prioritize LP income.
- **Profit Splits**
  Once the preferred return is met, profits are split—often 70/30 or 80/20 LP/GP.
- **Promote**
  This is the sponsor's bonus—earned only after hitting performance thresholds.

▶ **Red Flag: Sponsor Gets Paid First**
If the sponsor earns hefty acquisition fees, asset management fees, and promote *before* LPs receive preferred returns, the structure is out of balance. Ask:

- Is the preferred return cumulative?
- Is it compounding?
- Does the GP get a catch-up or waterfall bonus?

In a well-aligned deal, the sponsor only wins when you do.

4. Key Return Metrics You Should Know

Understanding these terms will make you a sharper LP overnight:

Metric	What It Measures
Cash-on-Cash	Annual income relative to capital invested
IRR	Time-weighted return (speed + size of return)
Equity Multiple	Total return over the full hold period

Why They Matter:

- **Cash-on-Cash** shows liquidity and cash flow strength.
- **IRR** shows velocity—how fast returns are realized.
- **Equity Multiple** shows total return—it's your bottom line.

▶ **Red Flag: Overreliance on IRR**
IRR can be manipulated. Sponsors often front-load distributions to inflate IRR or assume aggressive sale timelines that may not materialize. Always ask:

- What happens if the sale takes longer?
- What if we exit in a down market?

5. What Influences Your Return?

- **Asset Class**
  Core assets (Class A apartments, fully leased industrial) usually mean lower risk and lower return. Value-adds offer higher upside—and higher execution risk.

- **Financing Structure**
  Interest-only loans can inflate early returns but add refinance risk. Watch the loan maturity timeline.
- **Business Plan**
  Is the property being repositioned? Rebranded? Renovated? All of that affects risk and return timing.
- **Market Forces**
  Cap rates, interest rates, inflation, and local economic trends play a huge role in shaping final outcomes.

6. What's a "Good" Return?

Here's a general range for 5–7 year holds:

Return Type	Typical Range
Cash-on-Cash	6%–12% per year
IRR	12%–20% over hold period
Equity Multiple	1.5x–3.0x total return

Higher isn't always better. High returns often signal higher risk, aggressive projections, or loose underwriting.

The question isn't just "Is this return good?"
It's **"Is this return believable?"**

7. How to Evaluate a Deal Like a Pro

You don't need a finance degree to vet a deal. You just need discipline and a few key questions:

- Do the return projections match the business plan?
- Are exit assumptions based on cap rate compression—or reality?
- What if expenses rise faster than rents?
- Who gets paid if the property doesn't perform?

▶ **Red Flag: It Only Works in Excel**
Anyone can make a deal look great in a spreadsheet. The best sponsors know where the weak points are—and show their stress tests.

Ask them directly:

- What happens if rents only grow 2%?
- What if we exit in year 8 instead of 5?

If the deal still pencils, you're on solid ground.

8. How Sponsors Communicate Matters

Once you're in, you're blind without updates.

Great sponsors:

- Send detailed monthly or quarterly updates
- Report occupancy, NOI, leasing progress, and challenges
- Explain variance vs. budget clearly
- Admit when things go wrong

▶ **Red Flag: Radio Silence or Vague Reports**
If you can't tell what's happening—or the tone shifts from confident to cagey—you may be flying blind.

9. Case Studies: Real Deals, Real Red Flags

Case Study 1: The Illusion of Cash Flow

- **Pitch:** 9% preferred return from Day 1
- **Reality:** 40% vacancy, major deferred maintenance
- **What Happened:** Sponsor paid early distributions from reserves. Once those dried up, distributions stopped. NOI never caught up.
- **Red Flag:** Money showed up—before the property performed.

Case Study 2: The 80/20 That Cost LPs Everything

- **Pitch:** 2.5x equity multiple, 80/20 split after 8% preferred
- **Reality:** Sponsor stacked fees at every level—acquisition, development, construction management, asset management, disposition
- **What Happened:** Construction ran late. Costs ballooned. LPs got diluted while GPs still cashed in.
- **Red Flag:** The fee stack was heavier than the waterfall.

10. Bonus: Hidden Costs That Kill Returns

Returns are what's left—after the sponsor, lender, and property manager all take their share. Watch for:

- Acquisition Fees (1–5% of purchase price)
- Asset Management Fees (1–2% of gross income)
- Construction Management Fees (especially in value-add)
- Refinance Fees (often 1% of new loan)
- Disposition Fees (1–2% of sale price)

▶ **Red Flag: Death by a Thousand Fees**
If a sponsor can make six figures before the property stabilizes, ask how they're incentivized to stay long-term.

11. Return Illustration: 5-Year Example

Let's assume:

- Investment: $100,000
- Equity Multiple: 2.10x
- Total Return: $210,000
- IRR: ~17.5%

Year	Distribution	Cumulative	Notes
1	$6,000	$6,000	Lease-up phase
2	$8,000	$14,000	Full occupancy
3	$8,500	$22,500	Rent increases in effect
4	$9,000	$31,500	Cash-out refi prep
5	$178,500	$210,000	Final distribution from sale

Seems great. But ask:

- What happens if the sale takes two more years?
- What if the property appraises 10% lower than expected?

Stress test your optimism.

12. When Cash Flow Stops: What LPs Miss

What if cash flow slows or halts?

Most LPs panic.

But slow distributions don't always mean failure. They might signal:

- Reinvestment in operations
- Lease-up transition
- Seasonal fluctuations
- Renovation phase

The key is transparency.

▶ **Red Flag: No Explanation, Just Silence**
If distributions stop and updates disappear, that's when you worry. Good sponsors tell you what's happening before you ask.

13. Should You Reinvest Distributions?

Some sponsors offer the ability to reinvest your distributions into future deals. It's tempting, especially when returns are strong.

But remember:

- Reinvested capital often has no liquidity
- You may lose optionality
- Tax strategy could be impacted

Ask:
Is this compounding—or just convenience?

14. Is a Refinance a Return?

Sponsors often refinance properties midway through the hold period. This can return a chunk of your original capital—but it's not the same as profit.

A refinance is **debt**, not cash flow.

▶ **Red Flag: Refi Distributions Framed as "Profit"**
Understand:

- What terms the new debt carries
- Whether the loan adds long-term risk
- If a capital call might follow

15. Red Flags Recap—Chapter 4

1. Promising Day 1 Cash on a Heavy Lift – Where's the money really coming from?
2. Over-Optimistic Rent Projections – Validate with comps, not confidence.
3. Non-Cumulative Preferred Returns – The fine print matters.

4. Misaligned Incentives – Does the GP win when you lose?
5. Shiny IRRs Without a Solid Plan – What if the market shifts?
6. Fee Stack That Eats Returns – The structure should reward execution, not transactions.
7. Refis Masking Weak Performance – Debt ≠ profit.
8. Silence When Cash Flow Stops – Lack of transparency is its own answer.

Final Thought

Syndications can offer cash flow, tax advantages, and appreciation—but only if you understand how and when you're getting paid.

Ask the right questions. Check the assumptions. Verify the structure.

Because in passive investing, your greatest risk isn't the real estate—it's what you didn't ask.

Coming up next: What happens when deals exit—and how that outcome is shaped from Day 1.

Investor Dinner, Miami

CHAPTER 5
EXIT STRATEGIES—THE MOST OVERLOOKED RISK IN THE DEAL

Where Most Returns Are Made... or Lost

In this chapter, we'll break down the 5 most common exit strategies, the assumptions baked into each one, and the red flags that can wreck a good deal at the finish line.

Every syndication begins with a story about how it ends. Sponsors pitch a five-year timeline. A clean sale. Maybe a refinance around year three. A crisp 2x equity multiple with a 15%+ IRR. It sounds strategic. Predictable. Polished.

But here's the truth:
The exit is one of the riskiest, most unpredictable parts of the entire deal.

Why? Because you're betting on the future:

- That the market will stay strong
- That interest rates will cooperate
- That buyers will show up
- And that the sponsor's business plan executes on time and on budget

That's a lot of variables—and only a few are within your control.

1. Sale of the Property

What it is:
The sponsor improves the asset and sells it—ideally at a higher price than they bought it for.

Why it matters:
This is where the bulk of your profit lives. Distributions during the hold help, but equity at sale is often the primary driver of your overall return.

▶ **Red Flag: The Cap Rate Fantasy**
If the sponsor assumes they'll sell at a lower cap rate than they bought for, they're assuming the market improves over time. That's risky—especially in a rising interest rate environment.

What to ask:

- "What exit cap rate is being modeled?"
- "What if the cap rate increases by 0.5%?"

Just a small change in cap rate can wipe out a major chunk of your projected return.

2. Refinance

What it is:
The sponsor replaces the original loan with new debt at a higher valuation, returning some or all of your invested capital—without selling the property.

Why it matters:
It creates liquidity without a tax event. You can keep earning distributions while putting that returned capital into new deals.

▶ Red Flag: Refi Dependency

If the entire IRR or equity multiple hinges on a refinance happening at a specific time—with specific rates and values—that's not a strategy. That's a bet.

What to ask:

- "Does the business plan work without the refi?"
- "What's the backup if interest rates spike or NOI lags?"

If there's no margin of error, you're playing defense from Day 1.

3. Recapitalization

What it is:
The sponsor brings in new investors to buy out the original LPs. The property is held longer, but you get cashed out early—at a sponsor-determined valuation.

Why it matters:
It offers an off-ramp—even when the broader market isn't optimal for a sale.

▶ Red Flag: Valuation Vague Zone

Who sets the price? Is it an appraised value? Internal projection? Negotiated deal?
If it's unclear—or based on the sponsor's "opinion of value"—you're at a disadvantage.

What to ask:

- "How is the buyout value calculated?"
- "Do LPs have the right to an independent valuation?"
- "Is this a partial or full recap?"

Pro Tip: Recaps can be a smart tool—or a way for the sponsor to reset equity ownership in their favor.

4. 1031 Exchange

What it is:
Rather than taking cash at sale, the sponsor rolls proceeds into another property—allowing you to defer capital gains taxes under IRS Section 1031.

Why it matters:
It's one of the few ways to grow wealth without triggering a tax bill.

▶ Red Flag: 1031 Bait-and-Switch
Most syndications aren't structured for 1031s. LPs typically can't exchange their individual shares—they need the entire entity to participate.

What to ask:

- "Is this deal eligible for a 1031 rollover at exit?"
- "Can I opt out and take a cash payout?"
- "Has the sponsor done a successful 1031 in the past?"

If this strategy matters to you, don't assume—verify the structure before investing and consult a 1031 expert.

5. Hold and Cash Flow

What it is:
Instead of selling, the sponsor keeps the asset long-term, prioritizing stable income over a defined exit.

Why it matters:
For investors seeking passive income and tax deferral, this can be a great fit.

▶ Red Flag: No Liquidity, No Timeline

If your capital is tied up indefinitely, what's your plan if life changes? If the deal has no exit plan, make sure you're okay with a very long hold.

What to ask:

- "Is there a mechanism for LP buyouts?"
- "What's the communication cadence if the timeline changes?"

Real-World Example: The Refi That Never Came

A sponsor projected a 5-year hold with a refinance in Year 3 that would return 70% of investor capital. But interest rates doubled. The refi became impossible—and so did the projected IRR.

The sponsor had to pivot:

- Increased distributions from 6% to 8% annually to maintain investor trust
- Extended the hold period to 7 years
- Adjusted the equity multiple target downward

Investors still made money—but it was slower, less than expected, and tested everyone's patience.

The lesson: Always ask how the deal performs without the exit going perfectly.

Sponsor Language to Watch For in Pitch Decks

Sometimes, the red flags are in the wording:

- "We plan to refinance in Year 3" → Is that a plan or a requirement?
- "Targeted exit cap rate of 4.5%" → Why is that lower than today's market?

- "We expect a 1031 exchange opportunity" → Is it baked into the structure—or just an idea?
- "10% IRR even in conservative scenarios" → Ask to see those scenarios—don't just take their word for it.

What If You Need to Exit Early?

Syndications are typically illiquid investments.
When you commit capital, you're usually in for the full term—often 3 to 7 years.
But life happens. Priorities change. And sometimes, investors need a way out.

Can You Sell Early?
The short answer: sometimes.
Here are a few options that may be available—depending on the deal and sponsor:

Sponsor Buyback
Some sponsors offer buyback programs or will try to place your interest with another investor in the deal.
This isn't guaranteed, and the terms may not be favorable (you might sell at a discount), but it's one way to access liquidity.

Secondary Market Sale
In some cases, your ownership can be sold on a secondary market, especially if the offering was made under Regulation D and there's another interested accredited investor.
Again, this depends on the sponsor's structure and the operating agreement. Some sponsors allow it, some don't.

Operating Agreement Language
Always check the PPM (Private Placement Memorandum) and Operating Agreement for transfer restrictions. Some deals require sponsor approval for any transfer or sale. Others may impose a holding period before you can exit.

Bottom Line:

Before investing, ask the sponsor:

- "What happens if I need to exit early?"
- "Is there a buyback program or transfer process?"
- "Have other investors exited early before—and how did that go?"

Early exits aren't common, but they do happen.
The key is understanding your options before you need them.

Final Thought: Exit Risk Is Real

Sponsors love to pitch returns. But real investors understand how those returns happen—and what has to go right.

The best sponsors build deals that work even if:

- Cap rates go up
- Refis aren't possible
- The sale takes longer
- Buyer appetite softens

And they communicate clearly when conditions change.
The worst ones?
They disappear when Plan A fails—because they never had a Plan B.

▶ **Red Flags Recap: Exit Strategy Risk**

1. **Overly Optimistic Exit Cap Rates**
   A 0.5% shift can kill your profit. Challenge every assumption.
2. **Refinance Dependency**
   If the deal only works with a refi—run.
3. **Vague Recap Language**
   If the buyout terms aren't clear, you'll lose leverage when it counts.

4. **1031 Promises Without Structure**
   You can't retrofit a 1031. Confirm eligibility up front.
5. **No Liquidity in Long-Term Holds**
   Passive shouldn't mean "permanently stuck."

Like this book?
Leave a quick review!

Scan the QR code or visit:
https://www.amazon.com/dp/
B0FDWZK1Z3

Scroll down, and click
"Write a customer review".

PART III
PROTECTING YOUR CAPITAL

CHAPTER 6
HOW TO SCREEN DEALS WITHOUT GETTING BURNED

Control Happens Up Front—Or Not at All

Syndications are passive—but that doesn't mean they're hands-off. The moment you wire funds, you're locked in. You've effectively given up control. So the time to protect your downside isn't after you invest. It's before.
That's where your leverage lives.

Every experienced LP I know has the same war story: a deal they regret. A gut feeling they ignored. A sponsor they "really liked" who went dark when the numbers turned. But the lesson is always the same:

▶ **Red Flag: Passive Doesn't Mean Powerless**
You're not in control after the check clears. But before that? You're the most powerful person in the room.

This chapter is your pre-flight checklist.
Because the biggest risks in syndications don't come from the tenants. Or the economy. Or even the property.
They come from the decisions made before you ever see a dollar.

The Real Meaning of Control in a Syndication

You're not "giving up" control when you invest passively. You're choosing a different kind of control—the kind that happens before the deal.

You're exercising control by:

- Vetting the sponsor (before you trust them)
- Understanding the structure (before it locks you in)
- Stress-testing the business plan (before it becomes a real problem)

You're setting the terms of your future power—or powerlessness.
Once you're in, you're a passenger.
So your only chance to drive is before you board.

Why Most Mistakes Happen Before the Deal Closes

People say syndications are risky.
But the structure isn't the problem. The blind spots are.

Syndications offer real advantages:

- Diversification—Smaller checks across more markets
- Professional Execution—You're not fixing toilets, but someone better be
- True Passivity—If you pick the right operator

The risk comes when investors treat due diligence like a formality. When they see a webinar, glance at a slide deck, and assume the sponsor has it covered.

▶ **Red Flag: "This All Sounds Good" Isn't a Vetting Strategy**

The Red Flag Filter: A 4-Step System for Screening Deals

Over time, we've developed a simple four-part framework for screening deals. It helps us slow down. Clarify. Walk away from shaky structures.

And more than once—it's saved our capital.

Macro Tailwinds: Are You Betting With the Wind?

No deal exists in a vacuum.

Ask:
- Are interest rates rising or falling?
- What phase of the market cycle are we in?
- Is this asset class still healthy in this region?

Example:
In 2021, thousands of deals were underwritten with 3% exit cap rates and aggressive rent growth. In 2023, when cap rates hit 6–7%, many of those deals imploded.

▶ **Red Flag: Sponsors Who Act Like Macro Trends Don't Matter**
If the pitch doesn't acknowledge inflation, interest rate risk, or recession planning—it's not a pitch. It's a fairytale.

2. Operator Quality: Nothing Matters More

Asset quality matters. Market selection matters.
But nothing matters more than the person running the show.

Ask:
- Have they done this exact type of deal before?
- What's their communication style when things go wrong?
- Are they investing alongside you?

Real track record means exits. Cash-on-cash returns. Communication during the hard quarters—not just the highlight reels.

▶ Red Flag: "Co-GP" Setups With No Defined Roles
Watch for this pattern: an influencer raises capital and attaches themselves to a team they barely know. If the org chart looks like musical chairs, ask: who's really running the deal?

3. Downside Protection: Show Me the Floor

Everyone sells the upside. Few explain the floor.

You want to know:
- Breakeven occupancy – How low can occupancy fall before the deal bleeds?
- Capital reserves – Is there a real cushion for debt service or CapEx?
- Refi risk – If interest rates rise, can the deal still work?
- Extension options – What happens if they miss the projected exit window?

▶ Red Flag: They Dodge Questions or Sound Defensive
If you ask a reasonable question and get a vague answer—or a frustrated one—that's your answer.

4. Legacy & Wealth Preservation: Not Just a Payout—A Plan

Some investors chase IRR. That's fine.
But long-term wealth comes from durable cash flow, tax efficiency, and strategic hold periods—not just flipping for a gain.

Ask:
- Does this deal produce cash flow—or just appreciation?
- Is the depreciation structure clear?
- How does this fit into your timeline and strategy?

▶ **Red Flag: It's All Tax Talk, No Operational Plan**
If the first five minutes of the pitch are about bonus depreciation—and zero about leasing velocity or debt terms—you're being sold a tax shelter, not an investment.

Operator Red Flags to Watch For

Even a great property will fail with a poor operator.

Watch for:
- ▶ Poor Communication – If they're vague or dismissive now, imagine them in a crisis.
- ▶ Vague Business Plans – "We'll raise rents." Based on what? Without comps, it's fluff.
- ▶ No Track Record, All Hype – Energy ≠ execution. Charm doesn't pay distributions.
- ▶ No Downside Scenario – If you ask "What if this goes sideways?" and they deflect... run.

The 3 Most Dangerous Words in Due Diligence: "I Like Them"

Most investors never say it out loud.
But it's what they're really thinking when they gloss over underwriting. When they ignore weak comp data. When they forgive a sloppy deck or a missing PPM.

"I like them."

▶ **Red Flag: Personality Is Not Performance**
Ask yourself:
- Have I seen any hard evidence this person can execute?
- If I didn't like them, would I still back this deal?
- Would I trust them with $100K if they couldn't smile or sell?

Bet on competence, not charisma.

What About Liquidity?

Syndications are illiquid by design.
That's a feature, not a flaw.
You're locking capital away for 3-7 years in exchange for scale, tax advantages, and passive cash flow.

But still—ask:
- "Can I exit early?"
- "Is there a transfer process?"
- "Have past LPs exited mid-deal?"
- "Do they have a secondary market?"

▶ **Red Flag: Sponsors Don't Know—or Get Defensive About—Liquidity Terms**
If they can't explain how LP equity transfers work, they're not ready to handle capital at scale.

The Deal Room Trap: Urgency ≠ Alignment

You'll hear this a lot:
"We're closing fast. We just need your commitment."

Urgency is one of the most powerful tools in sales—and one of the biggest risks in private investing.

Ask:
- "When did the raise start?"
- "How many deals have they done this year?"
- "Are they raising to close—or scrambling to fill gaps?"

▶ **Red Flag: You Feel Pressured—Not Empowered**
A good sponsor wants educated investors.
A bad sponsor wants compliant ones.

Questions That Change the Conversation

Here's how to move from surface-level trust to strategic clarity.

Ask:
- "Can you walk me through your worst deal?"
- "How did you handle communication when COVID hit?"
- "What would success look like for you as a GP?"
- "What's your biggest operational blind spot?"

The goal isn't to be combative. It's to go beyond the pitch deck.

Bonus Filter: Incentives Tell the Truth

The capital stack tells a story. So do the fees.
- Do they earn a promote only after you hit your preferred return?
- Is the asset management fee based on gross revenue or net income?
- Who gets paid during a refinance?

▶ **Red Flag: Front-Loaded Fees or Guaranteed GP Income**
If the GP makes six figures before stabilization—and keeps earning during underperformance—that's not alignment. That's extraction.

Case Study: The Deal That Looked Great (Until It Didn't)

The Setup:
A multi-family value-add deal in Phoenix with a strong operator and great market data. With an 8% preferred return with a 2x equity multiple. Comps supported the rent bumps.

The Miss:
The sponsor had completed dozens of deals—but mostly as a co-GP. They were the lead operator on this one. No downside scenarios were modeled. They refinanced early... and rates jumped.

The Outcome:
NOI dropped. Cash flow dried up. Refinancing costs exploded. Distributions stopped. LPs were stuck with lower equity and zero communication.

What Was Missed:
- No real solo track record
- No sensitivity analysis
- GP incentives weren't tied to performance

Lesson: Even great markets and good properties fail without planning.

Stress Testing for LPs: The 6-Question Gauntlet

1. What's the worst-case scenario for this asset class right now?
2. What would happen if rents fell 10% and expenses rose 10%?
3. What does the capital stack look like if the refi fails?
4. How does the sponsor make money during hard times?
5. Who's running day-to-day operations, and can they be replaced?
6. What happens if the exit gets delayed by 2 years?

If you can't get straight answers to those—pause.

Tools You Should Actually Use

- SEC Enforcement Search – Look up the sponsor's name and firm: https://www.sec.gov/litigation
- Google Past Deal Names – Check for lawsuits, reviews, or court filings.
- Ask for References – Speak to current and former LPs.
- Review the PPM and Operating Agreement – Don't just "trust the lawyer."

▶ **Red Flag: Sponsor Pushback on Transparency**
You're not being difficult. You're being responsible.

Want the Full Checklist?

Want to stress-test your next deal with the same tools we use? Email me at carson@passive.investments or check out our LP Toolkit in the later chapters.

☑ Case Study: The Deal That Almost Didn't Happen (But Should Have)

The Setup:
A 96-unit apartment complex in North Carolina. The sponsor had a modest but verifiable track record. The market was growing: population, jobs, rents, all trending up. The returns were solid but not flashy: 6% pref, 1.8x equity multiple over 5 years.

Why We Almost Skipped It:
The webinar was underwhelming. The sponsor wasn't charismatic. Their deck was ugly. The rent bumps were conservative. It looked... boring.

What Made Us Say Yes:
- They answered every question with data, not spin.
- Their last five exits all beat pro forma.
- The model included a sensitivity table with downside scenarios.
- They personally invested $200K into the deal.

The Outcome:
Over three years, the deal hit nearly every milestone. Rents increased slowly but steadily. Expenses were tightly managed. Distributions started early and never missed a payment. When it exited in Year 4, we landed a 2.1x equity multiple—without the drama.

Lesson: Flashy sells. But boring often performs.

THE RED FLAG PLAYBOOK

The Sponsor Scorecard—A Tactical LP Filter

You don't need to be a forensic accountant to screen a deal. But you do need a system. Here's a simple 10-point Sponsor Scorecard you can adapt. Score each on a 1–5 scale:

☐ Sponsor Scorecard Table

Criteria	Poor	Average	Strong
Track Record	No exits	1-2 exits	Multiple full-cycle exits
Transparency	Vague answers	Some detail	Open, clear, frequent
Communication	Slow/inconsistent	Responsive	Proactive updates
Skin in the Game	0-3% of capital raised	3-5% of capital raised	5-10% of capital raised
Fees	High, layered	Standard	Low, aligned

▶ **Bonus Red Flags That Don't Seem Like Red Flags**

Some of the biggest warning signs are subtle. They don't scream "fraud." But they should raise your level of scrutiny.

1. Too Polished, No Substance
If the deck looks like it was made by a Madison Avenue ad agency—but you can't get a straight answer about who's operating the deal or how leasing will work—pause.
Polish ≠ plan.

2. "We Haven't Finalized That Yet"
If you're in a webinar and the sponsor says this more than once—about debt terms, CapEx scope, or fees—you're not early. You're uninformed. Capital shouldn't be raised on incomplete plans.

3. The Pro Forma Is "Dynamic"

Translation: they can change it later. If there's no locked model, no assumptions schedule, and you're being asked to wire funds... that's a hard pass.

Underwriting Wins vs. Gut Feelings

Your job as an LP isn't to find the "perfect" deal.
It's to systematically eliminate bad ones—and lean into good ones with your eyes open.

Good screening doesn't mean perfection. It means:

- Being able to explain why you passed
- Being able to justify why you said yes
- Never outsourcing judgment to charisma

Some of our best decisions came from saying "no" to big promises that didn't pencil out—even when we liked the sponsor.

And some of our best deals looked average on the surface but had discipline and operational clarity underneath.

◐ Know Your Rights: Capital Calls Aren't Always Wrong—But They Should Never Be a Surprise

Not all capital calls are red flags.
Some are triggered by valid issues: unexpected repair costs, slower-than-expected lease-ups, or lender requirements during tough market cycles.

But even when justified, capital calls create stress and potential consequences for passive investors. Before you invest, you need to understand not just why capital calls happen, but what your rights are when they do.

🚩 Common (Legitimate) Reasons for Capital Calls:

- Renovation overruns: The rehab budget was too tight or missed hidden issues.
- Operating shortfalls: Vacancy stayed high longer than projected.
- Emergency repairs or gaps in insurance coverage
- Loan covenant breaches: The lender requires more equity to stay in compliance.
- Avoiding a distressed sale: Sponsor wants to raise cash to hold the asset longer instead of selling at a loss.

Those are understandable, but here's the key:
A capital call should never catch you off guard.

Every investor should ask:
- Does the PPM or operating agreement even allow capital calls?
- Are you obligated to fund them—or can you opt out?
- What happens if you don't participate? Will your equity be diluted?
- Is the sponsor contributing their share—or just asking LPs to cover the gap?

And don't forget the context: some sponsors avoid raising adequate reserves upfront so their deal "pencils better" on paper.
But that's kicking the can down the road—until the road hits a wall.

When you see language about additional capital in the PPM, don't skim it. Highlight it. Ask about it. Understand it.
Because once the deal's in motion, your leverage as an LP shrinks fast.

🔚 Final Thoughts

You don't need to catch every red flag.
But you do need a process.

The best LPs aren't just skeptical—they're structured.
They don't invest because of FOMO or a fancy webinar.

They invest because they've walked a sponsor through the gauntlet, stress-tested the plan, and still liked what they saw.

This chapter isn't about saying no to everything.
It's about building conviction—or walking away with confidence.

Because once the money moves, the power shifts.
Before the wire? That's when you drive.

CHAPTER 7
THE RED FLAGS YOU CAN'T AFFORD TO MISS IN A SYNDICATION

Yes, syndications can build passive income. Yes, they can give you exposure to real estate without tenants, toilets, or 3 A.M. emergency calls. But let's be clear: Passive income isn't passive due diligence. Wire $50,000 or $100,000 into the wrong deal without doing your homework, and you're not investing—you're gambling.

This chapter is your early-warning system. The worst losses I've seen in this space didn't happen because of black swan events or macro crashes. They happened because of red flags that were visible—just ignored.

What follows aren't hypotheticals. These are the patterns that show up repeatedly in deals that go sideways. If you know what to watch for, you can avoid them before it's too late.

Root Causes of LP Blind Spots

Before we dive into the technical red flags, let's talk about the human side of investing.

The truth? Most LPs don't ignore red flags out of laziness. They miss them because of psychology:

- **Confirmation Bias:** If you like the sponsor, you subconsciously look for information that confirms your optimism.
- **FOMO:** Deals fill up quickly. Scarcity triggers urgency, and urgency lowers scrutiny.
- **Overreliance on "Referrals":** A trusted friend investing doesn't guarantee a deal is sound.
- **Tax-First Thinking:** Investors sometimes focus on depreciation benefits instead of fundamentals.

It's human nature to chase what feels good. But investing is about what works, not what feels right.
Systems beat emotion. Always.
When your brain says, "It'll probably be fine," your process should say, "Prove it."

▶ 1. Market Risk—Investing Blind to the Bigger Picture

The Setup: Everything looks great—until the local economy cracks. A major employer leaves, job growth stalls, or rent control laws are passed. Suddenly, your 18% IRR becomes a scramble for breakeven.

Red Flags to Watch:
- One-employer towns (military bases, manufacturing hubs, data centers)
- Buzzword-driven markets ("booming," "hot") with no hard migration, wage, or employment data
- Rent growth assumptions that outpace regional trends without explanation

🔍 **Smart Sponsors Ask:** "What happens if job growth slows?" "Are we overexposed to one employer or industry?"

🧠 **Investor Tip:** Always look up job growth and population trends yourself. Free resources like census data, Bureau of Labor Statistics, and U-Haul migration indexes can give you a rough but useful picture.

Real-World Miss: A Texas sponsor banked on continued Amazon expansion to support rent growth. They projected 6% annual increases for five years. Then Amazon froze hiring. Within 12 months, vacancy doubled. The IRR dropped to 6%.

Lesson: The market isn't the story—the fundamentals are.

▶ 2. Property Risk—The Ticking Time Bomb Beneath the Surface

The Setup: The listing says "light value-add." But after close, the plumbing fails, HVAC dies, or the tenant base proves far more volatile than promised. Suddenly, you're funding repairs instead of collecting cash flow.

Red Flags:
- No PCA (Property Condition Assessment)
- CapEx budget that feels thin or "TBD"
- Photos that skip problem areas
- Claims of "cosmetic only" renovations with no inspection backup

What to Ask: "When were the roof, plumbing, and HVAC last replaced?" "Was a third-party inspection completed and shared?"

Investor Tip: Ask to see before-and-after photos of similar past projects. If a sponsor can't show they've executed upgrades well before, why trust they'll do it now?

Real-World Miss: A self-storage deal closed without a PCA to "move fast." Within three months, $180,000 in unbudgeted roofing costs halted distributions—and triggered a capital call.

Lesson: You're not buying a brochure. You're buying a building—with problems included.

▶ 3. Sponsor Risk—The Operator Is the Deal

The Setup: A mediocre property with a strong sponsor can survive. A great property with a weak or dishonest sponsor? That's a ticking bomb.

Red Flags:
- No personal investment ("skin in the game")
- Avoidance or vague answers when questioned
- Promising "no downside" or "we've never missed projections"
- Defensive or slick when discussing past performance

🔍 **What to Ask:** "Tell me about a deal that didn't go to plan." "Can I speak with an LP from a deal that underperformed?"

💬 **Bonus Tip:** Google them. Check litigation history. Ask your CPA or attorney to check them out. One lawsuit may be noise. Multiple? That's a a red flag.

⚠ **Mini Warning Sign:** "We've never had a deal underperform." That's either a lie—or they've only done one deal.

Lesson: Underwrite the sponsor before you underwrite the asset. They are your business partner.

▶ 4. Structural Risk—Death by Fine Print

The Setup: The equity split sounds great—until you see the waterfall. LPs are last in line, buried under fees and promotes.

Structural Red Flags:
- No preferred return—or it's non-cumulative
- Aggressive catch-up clauses
- High acquisition, asset management, and exit fees
- Preferred equity or mezz debt ahead of common LPs

🔍 **What to Ask:** "Is the pref cumulative and compounding?" "What's the total sponsor fee load as a percent of revenue?"

💡 **Investor Tip:** If the deal has a waterfall, ask for a flowchart. If they can't explain it in plain English, they're either confused—or hiding something.

Real-World Miss: A sponsor touted an 8% pref with an 80/20 split. But they stacked $400K in annual fees—before LPs saw a dime. The sponsor got rich. The investors barely cleared 3%.

Lesson: If the structure pays the sponsor regardless of performance, you're not a partner—you're a donor.

▶ 5. Return Assumption Risk—The Best-Case Scenario Trap

The Setup: The numbers look amazing—on the spreadsheet. But they only work if everything goes right, all the time.

Red Flags:
- Rent increases that outpace the market without comps
- Cap rate compression baked in during rising rate cycles
- Unrealistic refinance assumptions

🔍 **What to Ask:** "What's the downside case IRR if rents stay flat?" "What's the cap rate sensitivity at exit?"

💡 **Stress Test It:** Ask the sponsor for a "downside" or "stress" case scenario—and make sure they actually have one.

Mini Test: Bump the exit cap rate by 1% or hold rents flat. If the IRR tanks, the model isn't resilient—it's fragile.

Lesson: Great deals survive bad years. Fragile ones need perfection.

▶ 6. Liquidity Risk—You're in Until You're Out

The Setup: Life changes. You want to exit the deal. But syndications are illiquid by design—most lock you in for 5 to 7 years.

Red Flags:
- Promises of "quarterly liquidity" with no process
- No internal transfer policy or secondary market plan

🔍 **What to Ask:** "What happens if I need to exit early?" "Have any LPs successfully sold their position before?"

💡 **Investor Tip:** Ask how many LPs have requested early exits. If it's a common issue, it may reflect deeper problems with deal quality or communication.

Lesson: Liquidity is possible, but never guaranteed. Only invest capital you can part with for the full term.

▶ 7. Tax Surprises—When Depreciation Doesn't Deliver

The Setup: Sponsors lead with tax benefits: bonus depreciation, paper losses, passive income. But recapture and sale impact are often downplayed.

Red Flags:
- Overpromising tax savings without explaining recapture
- No clarity on K-1 allocations or exit tax impact

🔍 **What to Ask:** "Will you provide a cost segregation study and depreciation schedule?" "What's the estimated tax liability from depreciation recapture at sale?"

💡 **Investor Tip:** If a sponsor can't explain recapture in under two minutes, they may not fully understand the tax consequences themselves.

Lesson: Taxes are a bonus, not a strategy. The deal still has to work on fundamentals.

▶ 8. No Margin for Error—The Invisible Cushion

The Setup: The deal pencils—but barely. If anything slips, it unravels.

Red Flags:
- No working capital reserves
- Construction or lease-up without contingency
- Sponsors who dismiss risk with "We'll figure it out"

🔍 **What to Ask:** "What's the breakeven occupancy and NOI?" "How much runway do you have if things go off-plan?"

💡 **Investor Tip:** Look for at least 5–10% contingency in CapEx and 6–12 months of operating reserves on value-add projects.

Lesson: Optimism doesn't pay bills. Liquidity and planning do.

⚠ Additional Red Flags LPs Overlook

- **Unvetted Third Parties:** Who's managing the property? Who's handling construction? If the sponsor shrugs, walk away.
- **Sponsor Turnover:** High internal churn may signal deeper dysfunction.
- **Overbranding and Flash:** A pitch deck that looks like a VC pitch may be heavy on story, light on substance.
- **Conflict of Interest:** Sponsors who also own the vendor companies (construction, management) may prioritize their profit over LP returns.

Real-World Case Studies: What I Wish I Saw

Case Study 1: A sponsor promised a 20% IRR with "light renovations." But they had no construction team and outsourced every contractor. Cost overruns destroyed margins.
▶ Missed: No execution infrastructure.

Case Study 2: A multifamily deal in the Midwest boasted "great demographics," but the town's population was shrinking. The sponsor used five-year-old census data.
▶ Missed: No current migration analysis.

Case Study 3: A storage facility pitched 9% day-one cash flow. In reality, the occupancy was propped up by month-to-month freebies.
▶ Missed: No audit of actual revenue.

The Red Flag Interview—10 Questions Every LP Should Ask

1. Tell me about a deal that didn't go as planned.
2. How do you get paid—and when?
3. Who's on your operating team, and can they be fired?
4. Have you ever issued a capital call?
5. What happens if the refinance fails?
6. Is the preferred return cumulative?
7. What's your average communication cadence with LPs?
8. Do you invest your own money in every deal?
9. How do you underwrite exit cap rate?
10. Can I talk to 2–3 LPs from past deals—including one that underperformed?

Final Word: Risk Isn't the Enemy—Ignoring It Is

Syndications don't fail overnight.
They crack, then crumble—slowly.
The best LPs aren't gamblers. They're pattern readers.
They catch misalignment before it becomes misfortune.

They ask the questions sponsors don't expect. And they listen closely when the answers get fuzzy.

Say "No" early so you never have to say "I wish I had."

● **The ultimate red flag? Confidence without transparency.**

CHAPTER 8
WHEN THINGS GO SIDEWAYS— RED FLAGS IN THE ROUGH

Every pitch deck tells a beautiful story. Projections climb. Photos shine. Bullet points brag. It all looks clean.

But no deal ever plays out exactly like the deck.
Not one.

Markets shift. Interest rates spike. Tenants pull out. Contractors flake. Insurance costs double. Renovations run long. And suddenly, that "bulletproof" pro forma looks like a coloring book drawn in crayon.

The question isn't if something will go wrong. The question is how prepared the sponsor is when it does—and how quickly they respond.

This chapter is about those moments when things go sideways. Not the glossy pitch, but the gritty in-between. The part where deals either recover—or unravel.

Because syndications aren't just about return potential. They're about risk management. And when things go sideways, the red flags start waving fast.

▶ Why Projections Miss—And What That Reveals

Every projection is a hypothesis. And like all hypotheses, they're tested the moment reality shows up.

1. Market Shocks
Inflation spikes. Interest rates rise. A major employer shuts down. Rent growth stalls or reverses. Suddenly the numbers don't just miss—they collapse.
Red Flag: A business plan that only works in blue-sky scenarios. If the deal only works when every variable aligns perfectly, it's not a business plan—it's a fantasy.

2. Surprise Expenses
Maybe the sponsor skipped a proper inspection. Maybe they underestimated the renovation scope. Or maybe, they didn't build in any buffer.
A single $150,000 surprise (roof, HVAC, code violations, etc.) can derail distributions for 12 months.
Red Flag: No contingency line item—or one that's clearly just for show. Ask: "What's the reserve per door? Per square foot?" If the answer sounds like a rounding error, it probably is.

3. Operational Breakdown
The deal gets acquired. Then nothing happens. Leasing slows. Repairs get delayed. Turnover rises. Property management flounders.
Red Flag: No named property manager in the plan—or no backup plan if they underperform. Sponsors love to say they're "vertically integrated." That sounds great... until you realize that means their cousin is running ops.

4. Aggressive Assumptions
Rents grow 6% annually. Cap rates compress magically. Expenses stay flat. And refi rates somehow remain stuck in 2021.

Red Flag: Every number assumes the best. Good sponsors stress-test their deals. Great ones show you the downside IRR and break-even scenarios.

5. Sponsor Distraction

Instead of fixing the deal, the sponsor's off raising money for the next one. They're doing webinars, podcasts, maybe even starting a fund.
Red Flag: More LinkedIn posts than property updates. If asset management takes a back seat to branding, you're a photo op—not a partner.

🧠 What Great Sponsors Do When It Hits the Fan

Here's the difference between a deal that survives turbulence—and one that implodes: how the sponsor responds when things go off-track.

☑ **They Communicate—Honestly and Early**
They don't ghost you. They don't sugarcoat the problem. They send detailed updates with real numbers and revised strategies.
Red Flag: Fluffy updates with no financials or hard data. Or worse—radio silence.

☑ **They Pivot—Fast and Transparently**
Markets change? They change with them. They push back CapEx. They renegotiate insurance. They shift leasing tactics.
Red Flag: "We're staying the course"... even when the course leads off a cliff.

☑ **They Use Reserves Strategically**
They planned for this. And when the storm comes, they deploy contingency capital the way a pilot lowers landing gear—not with panic, but precision.
Red Flag: "We'll figure it out later" = they already don't have a plan.

☑ **They Take the Hit First**

Sponsors with integrity stop taking fees before cutting investor distributions. They delay their promote. They lead by example.
Red Flag: Sponsor still collecting fees while LPs get zero.

☑ They Ask for Help
No one has all the answers. Smart operators have advisors, mentors, and veteran partners on speed dial.
Red Flag: Blaming the Fed, the tenants, the market—anything but their own plan.

👀 What YOU Should Do When Things Get Messy

You're passive—but that doesn't mean powerless.

📫 Stay Engaged
Read every update. Review the financials. Ask questions. Sponsors who welcome scrutiny are the ones you want to stay with.

🔍 Ask These Questions:
- What has changed from the original business plan?
- What adjustments have you made?
- Is the exit timeline shifting? Why?
- Have reserves been tapped? What's left?
- Are fees still being paid to the sponsor?

If the answers feel vague, avoidant, or overly polished—that's your answer.

🚶 Know When to Wait—and When to Walk
Some setbacks are recoverable. But a pattern of evasive communication, poor planning, and failure to adapt? That's not a rough patch—it's a red flag parade.

Know your rights in the operating agreement. If the sponsor won't provide updates or financials, you may need to lawyer up—or start organizing other LPs.

✵ Lessons from Deals That Didn't Go as Planned

Syndications don't blow up overnight. They erode. Slowly. Until one day the damage is visible.

Here's what failed deals can teach us all:
- Underwriting is everything. The most important number is the break-even IRR.
- Communication = trust. A sponsor who's clear in crisis is gold.
- Diversification isn't optional. Don't go all-in on a single "can't-miss" opportunity.
- Red flags multiply. One bad sign is a warning. Three is a pattern.

⚠ Mini Case Study: The Vanishing Update

In early 2022, a sponsor raised capital for a value-add multifamily deal with 18% projected IRR. The market was hot. The property had "easy upside." Investors bought in quickly.

By Q2 2023, distributions stopped. Leasing was behind. Expenses were up. But the real issue?
No updates.

LPs had no idea what was going on. Emails went unanswered. The sponsor resurfaced with a two-sentence note and no financials. When pressed, they insisted they were "staying the course."

What had gone wrong?
- They had no reserve budget.
- The refinance assumption was based on 2021 rates.
- They burned cash chasing performance bonuses—and got burned themselves.

The real red flag? Silence.

🔊 Bonus: The Post-Mortem Playbook

If you do find yourself in a troubled deal, use it as a masterclass.

Ask:
- What early clues did I ignore?
- What questions didn't I ask?
- Was I too focused on the return and not the risk?

Write it down. Share it with other LPs. Turn one painful deal into a checklist that protects you in the future.

If the sponsor comes back with another deal? Ask:
Did they take responsibility? Did they learn anything?
Did they take care of LPs even when it hurt?
Great sponsors aren't perfect. But they own their mistakes. Loudly.

☑ Case Study: The Sponsor Who Turned It Around

The Setup:
A 52-unit property in Alabama, purchased in early 2022 with a clear value-add strategy: light unit renovations, increased rents, and improved marketing. Then inflation hit. Insurance costs jumped 40%. Property taxes were reassessed. Rents weren't rising fast enough to offset it.

The Response:
- Within two weeks of realizing NOI was dipping below projections, the sponsor sent a detailed investor update.
- They paused all distributions immediately—not after running out of money, but in anticipation.
- They provided a new 12-month plan with adjusted CapEx, leasing goals, and reserve projections.
- Most importantly: they hosted a live Zoom call, took every question, and followed up with meeting notes and updated financials.

The Outcome:
The sponsor stabilized cash flow by deferring some non-essential renovations, re-negotiated property management contracts, and offered new lease incentives.

They didn't "save the day" in 30 days—but over 12 months, the property stabilized, NOI recovered, and LP trust stayed intact.

The Lesson:
The best sponsors don't promise perfection. They show you the playbook when things get messy—and then they run the play.

What Bad Communication Actually Looks Like

When things go wrong, sponsors often default to vague updates that sound positive but say nothing.

Here's a real (but anonymized) email excerpt an LP received when a deal hit trouble:

Subject: Q3 Update – Staying the Course!

"Hi everyone!
We've had a busy quarter with lots of moving pieces. The market continues to shift, but we remain optimistic and committed to our original vision.
Our team is working diligently to navigate some short-term turbulence. More updates soon—thanks for your continued support!"

There were no financials, no discussion of occupancy or revenue, and no mention of whether distributions were still coming.
It's the real estate version of, "Thoughts and prayers."
▶ **Red Flag:** Fluff + optimism = no plan.

📋 The Sponsor Crisis Response Checklist

Want to know if your sponsor is serious when things get hard? Run their behavior through this 5-point filter:

Category	What to Look For	Red Flag
Updates	Full transparency, with data and context	Vague emails, missing P&L or balance sheet
Strategy	Clear changes made in response to problems	"Staying the course" despite red numbers
Tone	Honest, direct, and confident—not defensive	Dismissive, overly optimistic, or condescending
Leadership	Sponsors take a pay cut before LPs do	Still collecting fees while distributions are paused
Engagement	Proactive communication—invites LP questions	Avoidant or unresponsive to follow-ups

If they fail 3+ of these? It's time to escalate—or exit.

🧐 Extra LP Power Moves When a Deal Goes Sideways

If you're in a deal that's struggling, here's how to turn passive into proactive:

1. **Request a Zoom Call**
   You're an investor—not an inconvenience. If communication is sparse, organize a group of LPs and ask for a 30-minute call. Good sponsors will show up.
2. **Review the Operating Agreement Again**
   Know your rights. Some agreements allow LPs to remove a GP with a supermajority. Others restrict communication. Don't assume—Read.
3. **Log All Sponsor Communication**
   Keep every email, every update, every timeline change. If the deal fully collapses, that record becomes evidence.

4. **Ask for a Third-Party Audit**
   If trust is eroding, suggest bringing in a third-party accountant to audit operations or verify financials. A professional operator won't resist.
5. **Educate, Don't Just React**
   Every messy deal teaches you something. Create your own post-mortem deck: what signals were missed, what questions went unasked, what you'll do differently next time.

⌀ The Real Cost of Silence

Bad deals rarely explode—they leak.
One sponsor we encountered paused distributions, stopped sending updates, and gave no heads-up before refinancing at a much worse rate. The LPs found out after it happened.

Even if the deal eventually recovers, trust never does.
When a sponsor chooses silence, they're not just hiding the problem—they're signaling that LPs don't matter.
And if you're invisible during the storm, you'll be forgotten in the outcome.

△ Final Word: Adversity Reveals Alignment

Anyone can look good when the deal is humming. But when it hits the fan, you see who's real—and who's just collecting checks.

This is where most passive investors lose money: not because they picked the wrong asset class, but because they trusted the wrong operator when the pressure mounted.

You don't need a crystal ball to avoid bad outcomes. You need:

- A plan before the wire
- A playbook when things get rocky
- The discipline to walk when trust breaks

Because syndications aren't just spreadsheets and tax benefits;
They're partnerships.
And when things go sideways, the character of your partner matters more than any cap rate on a deck.

CHAPTER 9
RED FLAGS IN THE REARVIEW

Horror Stories Every LP Should Learn From (So You Don't Star in Your Own)

Some of the best lessons in investing don't come from what went right. They come from what went very wrong.
The stories that stick with you aren't always the big wins. They're the deals that fell apart slowly, publicly, and painfully,—where red flags were flapping from the start, but no one wanted to acknowledge them. This chapter isn't about fear. It's about pattern recognition. These are real stories, drawn from real deals, that reveal what many LPs don't learn until they've already wired the money:
▶ Red flags are rarely hidden. They're ignored.
Read these carefully. Learn from other people's scars so you don't have to earn your own.

⚠ **Horror Story #1: The "Can't-Miss" Multifamily Deal That Missed Everything**

The Setup:
The pitch was flawless. High IRR. Fast turnaround. Experienced team (supposedly). The sponsor had charisma, momentum, and a social media presence that made it look like they were on a rocket ship. But they'd never taken a deal full cycle.

The investors ignored the gut check because they liked the energy. Investors Assumed: "They've raised this much capital—they must know what they're doing."
They didn't.

The Red Flags Missed:

- No sensitivity analysis in the underwriting
- No actual exit history, just "relevant experience"
- Sponsor focused more on brand-building than operations
- Vague answers to direct questions about reserves and debt structure
- No third-party construction oversight or renovation plan beyond "We've got this"

The Fallout:
Rents didn't hit target. Renovations dragged. Distributions dried up within six months. Then came the silence.
No updates. No quarterly financials. Just "we're working on it."
The deal eventually sold—at a loss. Not catastrophic, but painful.

The Lesson:
Confidence ≠ competence.
Charisma isn't a strategy.

Lessons for Next Time:

- Require full-cycle experience on at least 3 exits
- Ask for project photos and financials from previous deals—not just IRR claims
- Demand clear, written communication protocols
- Only invest with sponsors who send full quarterly reports with balance sheets and rent rolls
- If the sponsor won't put 6+ figures of their own capital in? I walk

🚩 Horror Story #2: The "Off-Market Steal" with a Toxic Surprise

The Setup:
An industrial asset in a hot logistics corridor. The broker called it a "unicorn" off-market deal. Sponsor said we had to move fast—before it hit the market and competition drove up the price.
Speed killed diligence.
We were told everything checked out. But there was a pending environmental concern buried in the title docs—one that required a Phase II environmental review.
The sponsor skipped it. "We're confident," they said. "It's standard industrial. We've done this before."
Turns out the site was a former automotive paint facility. Soil contamination. EPA oversight. Surprise!

The Red Flags Missed:

- Sponsor pressured for fast funding without final docs
- No finalized third-party reports provided pre-close
- Environmental risk was minimized, not investigated
- No legal review of title before closing
- "Trust us" was the primary diligence strategy

The Fallout:
Cleanup costs wiped out any chance of hitting pro forma returns. Operating income got crushed. Tenants pushed back. The sponsor eventually refinanced to return some capital—but nobody made a profit. Some LPs lost 30-40%.

The Lesson:
If diligence isn't complete, the deal isn't ready.
Urgency is not your friend.

Lessons for Next Time:

- Require complete and final third-party reports before wiring funds
- Insist on Phase I and, if flagged, Phase II environmental studies
- Read the title work—or have someone I trust read it
- Ask the sponsor, "What was the worst thing you uncovered during diligence?"

🏈 Horror Story #3: The Unverifiable Track Record

The Setup:
A fund manager with a flashy website, a slick pitch deck, and a long list of "successful exits." But when pressed, things got fuzzy.
Deals were "part of a joint venture." Results were "confidential." LP references were "limited due to privacy."
Investors went in anyway. Big mistake.

The Red Flags Missed:

- No written performance data—just anecdotes
- Every success story started with "I was involved in..." but no verification
- Sponsors avoided hard questions with charm or technical jargon
- No in-house accounting or investor relations team
- Background check showed a dissolved LLC in another state—but we dismissed it

The Fallout:
The fund stalled. Distributions stopped. The sponsor went quiet. After a year of ducking calls, investors learned he'd launched another fund—under a different entity.
The first fund? Still in limbo.

The Lesson:
You're not just vetting the numbers.

You're vetting the narrative.

Lessons for Next Time:

- Ask for a deal matrix: project name, projected vs. actual returns, exit dates
- Call at least two LPs from older deals—not just the current raise
- If something feels off—run background checks on all GPs
- Verify returns via closing statements or K-1s—not just claims in a pitch deck

🚩 Horror Story #4: The Refinance Mirage

The Setup:
The plan was to buy, renovate, and refinance at a lower interest rate.
The sponsor sold it hard: "We'll return most of your capital in Year 2."
But interest rates rose. Then they rose again.
The refinance became impossible.

The Red Flags Missed:

- Pro forma baked in a refinance at aggressive interest rates
- No "Plan B" if rates didn't cooperate
- Value-add assumptions relied on rapid rent hikes
- No stress test on the debt service coverage ratio

The Fallout:
The debt became unmanageable. Distributions paused. Capital calls loomed. Eventually, the sponsor was forced to sell—during a soft market.
The returns? Barely break-even. Some LPs walked away with less than they put in.

The Lesson:
Refinance is not a guaranteed exit.
It's a gamble—and the lender always wins first.

Lessons for Next Time:

- Ask: "Can this deal cash flow without a refi or sale?"
- Ignore refinance projections in return metrics
- Look for interest rate hedges or fixed-rate debt
- Demand a downside scenario that includes holding to maturity

👥 Horror Story #5: The Hidden JV Partner

The Setup:
The deal looked good. The sponsor was responsive, the deck was clean, and the business plan seemed solid. What investors didn't know? They weren't the only decision-maker.
A silent JV partner held a controlling interest—and a checkered legal history.

The Red Flags Missed:

- Only one name on the pitch deck—but two names in the operating agreement
- No disclosure of the JV structure in the investor call
- Partner had veto rights on capital events—but wasn't part of any LP communication
- Google search of the JV partner's name showed lawsuits we ignored

The Fallout:
When the market tightened, the JV partner blocked a much-needed refinance. The operator had no control. LPs were caught in the middle.
The deal dragged out and ultimately defaulted.

The Lesson:
If you don't know who's in control, you're not investing—you're speculating.

Lessons for Next Time:

- Ask: "Who has final authority over key decisions?"
- Read the operating agreement for hidden partners
- Google every name—Twice
- Ask: "Have you ever had a dispute with a JV partner?" and wait for the pause

🛡 My LP Operating System: How I Filter Deals Now

I don't just screen deals—I screen people. Here's the lens I now apply to every opportunity:

☑ **Sponsor Discipline**
Do they overcommunicate when things go wrong—or disappear?
▶ Red Flag: Smooth during fundraising, silent after funding.

☑ **Alignment of Interests**
Are LPs paid first? Is the sponsor willing to cut fees if the deal underperforms?
▶ Red Flag: GP gets paid regardless of results.

☑ **Founder Mindset**
Is this sponsor building a long-term platform—or chasing short-term wins?
▶ Red Flag: Flashy social media, constant raises, no operational focus.

☑ **Operational Depth**
Do they have a real team? Property managers? Controllers? Are they scaling carefully or recklessly?
▶ Red Flag: One-person show or revolving door of junior hires.

☑ **Deal Structure Transparency**
Do they lay out the waterfall clearly? Show fee schedules? Address downside scenarios in writing?
▶ Red Flag: "Don't worry, we'll take care of it."

☑ **Capital Stack Clarity**
Who else is in the deal, and in what position?
▶ Red Flag: Surprise mezzanine debt or preferred equity in front of you.

> ⚔ **Horror Story #6: The CapEx Fantasy**

The Setup:
A self-storage deal in the Midwest. The sponsor promised "light renovations" and value-add upside through better management, repainting, and a new gate system. It sounded simple. Bulletproof, even. But no CapEx schedule was ever shared. The quote for renovations was a single round number: $250K. No breakdown. No bids. No timeline.

The Red Flags Missed:

- No vendor quotes or CapEx detail in the data room
- Sponsor used the same renovation budget for three different properties
- "Soft commitments" from contractors—not hard bids
- No construction manager on staff or retainer
- No clear plan for phasing the upgrades

The Fallout:
Contractors didn't show. The gate upgrade was delayed 8 months. Marketing campaigns launched before the property was clean. Occupancy dropped. Collections worsened. And when a real property manager was finally brought in, it was too late to recapture momentum.

The Lesson:
The business plan is only as good as the execution plan—and execution starts with verified CapEx.

Lessons for Next Time:

- Require line-item CapEx budget with timestamps

- Ask for the construction phasing plan before wiring funds
- Ask: "Have these contractors worked with you before?"
- Ask: "What happens if you're 90 days behind on CapEx?" and watch how they answer

📖 Horror Story #7: The "We're Raising As We Go" Project

The Setup:
A ground-up development deal with 200+ units. Great location. Clean deck. And a sponsor with a smooth pitch: "We've got the land, we've got the entitlements—just need to fill the rest of the raise to break ground." They had raised half. The other half? "In progress."

The Red Flags We Missed:

- No committed capital for vertical construction
- Entitlements were "expected any week"
- Multiple webinars—but no hard timeline
- The raise had been open for six months already
- The sponsor didn't have the liquidity to cover gaps

The Fallout:
Construction costs jumped mid-raise. Steel and lumber surged. Permits were delayed. Capital never fully came in. So the project stalled—land sitting idle. Eventually, the sponsor had to sell the land to recoup partial LP capital.

The Lesson:
If the capital stack isn't closed, the deal isn't real.

Lessons for Next Time:

- Ask: "Is the entire raise committed or conditional?"
- Avoid development deals without 100% equity in hand
- Ask for a full draw schedule and capital timeline

- Watch for "rolling raises" that stretch 6+ months with no construction start

💭 LP Post-Mortem Template: Turn Pain Into Process

After every deal—good, bad, or breakeven—you should run a deal debrief. Here's how to do it:

1. Red Flag Reflection
    - What red flags did I see but rationalize?
    - Where did I trust my gut—and where did I override it?
    - Did I verify the sponsor's claims—or just believe them?

2. Underwriting Hindsight
    - Were projections too aggressive in hindsight?
    - Was the refi, exit, or rent growth plan realistic?
    - Did I factor in interest rate or expense sensitivity?

3. Sponsor Evaluation
    - How was communication during tough quarters?
    - Did they take responsibility—or make excuses?
    - Would I invest with them again?

4. Process Audit
    - Did I follow my own checklist?
    - What questions did I not ask?
    - Did I let urgency, trust, or branding cloud my judgment?

5. Portfolio Fit
    - Did this deal fit my actual goals—or just seem exciting?
    - Was I overexposed to a single sponsor or asset class?
    - How did this deal complement or complicate my portfolio?

☑ **Pro tip:** Keep a "Deal Journal" where you log key metrics, red flags, and personal takeaways after every investment. Over time, this becomes your most valuable resource—not just for screening sponsors, but for refining your strategy.

🧩 BONUS: Add These to Your Deal Filter

Every LP has their own style, but here are a few more filters I've added over time:

- **The Monthly Update Test**
  Ask: "Can I see a sample monthly report?" If they don't have one—or it's all fluff—expect the same post-close.
- **The Recession Test**
  Ask: "What's the worst economic event your team has operated through?" Listen for specifics. If they say, "We've stress tested the model," press for proof.
- **The Fee Test**
  Ask: "What fees do you collect before the LP sees a dime?" If the list is long and front-loaded, the deal is already misaligned.
- **The Fire Drill Test**
  Ask: "Tell me about a time your deal hit a wall. What did you do?" Their answer shows whether they operate—or just pitch.

🎯 Final Word: Learn to Run Toward the Wreckage

Great investors don't just remember the wins. They study the wreckage.

Not to dwell—but to build pattern recognition. Because every bad deal is a free education you paid a premium for.
If you use it, you grow. If you ignore it, you repeat it.

That's the hard truth of passive investing: you can't avoid all losses, but you can avoid the same losses.
Every LP horror story in this chapter had signs. They weren't subtle. They weren't hidden. They were visible.
Now you've seen them too.

You don't need a finance degree to avoid red flags.
You just need to remember the scars—and stay disciplined when the next "can't-miss" deal shows up in your inbox.

📖 Bonus Case: The Empty Deal Room

A newer investor shared this with me:
"The sponsor had a Dropbox folder with five files. That was it. No underwriting model. No third-party reports. The PPM was generic. I asked for more. They said, 'We're finalizing it next week—don't worry.'"
He wired $100K anyway.
No distributions. No reporting. No recourse.
The deal's still active... technically. But it's not performing. And the sponsor? Has gone quiet.

Lesson: If the data room is empty, the diligence is fake.

🧠 LP Post-Mortem Template: Learn From Every Deal

After a deal closes—win or lose—ask yourself:

- What red flags did I see but dismiss?
- What assumptions proved wrong?
- What did I learn about this sponsor's communication?
- What would I do differently in the next deal?
- Did I follow my own rules—or make exceptions?

Your investment losses can be expensive tuition. But if you reflect honestly, they don't have to be wasted.

🎯 Final Word: Your Greatest Risk Isn't the Deal—It's the Operator

When syndications go bad, they rarely implode overnight.
They erode—through poor communication, rushed diligence, misaligned incentives, and unqualified sponsors who know how to pitch but not how to operate.

The common thread across all these horror stories?
Someone ignored the signs.
The pitch sounded good. The sponsor was charming. The deck looked great.
And then it didn't.

If you take one thing from this chapter, make it this:
Don't back deals. Back people.
Because the right sponsor can salvage a struggling property.
But the wrong one can ruin a great one.

Syndications aren't a gamble when you do the work upfront.
The trick is spotting the danger early—in the documents, the interviews, the missing answers—and walking away before it becomes your problem.

The goal isn't to avoid every risk.
It's to avoid the predictable ones.
▶ Red flags aren't subtle. You just have to look.

**Like this book?
Leave a quick review!**

**Scan the QR code or visit:
https://www.amazon.com/dp/
B0FDWZK1Z3**

**Scroll down, and click
"Write a customer review".**

PART IV
CAPITAL, STRATEGY, AND ASSET CLASSES

CHAPTER 10
RED FLAGS IN CAPITAL RAISING

Why Most Investors Say "No"—and How to Earn Their Trust

Raising capital isn't about charisma. It's about alignment, transparency, and education. Most investors aren't skeptical because they're difficult—they're skeptical because they're uncertain. They've worked hard to build their wealth and don't want to see it vanish in a deal they didn't fully understand.

That's why education is your edge.

Whether you're raising your first $500K or structuring an eight-figure fund, your ability to explain—not just excite—determines how much capital you raise and how confidently it comes in.

The Early Days: Hustle, Not Leverage

My capital-raising journey didn't begin with fund structures and investor decks. It started at tables and booths—investment expos in Vegas, Houston, Florida—trying to explain deals one person at a time.

I scraped together $500K here, $1M there—just enough to cross the finish line.

One raise nearly broke me: a $3M raise where I personally pulled in the first $1.2M. But I ran out of bandwidth, fast. I was stuck in follow-up purgatory—no CRM, no automation, just hope and hustle.

What saved it? Partnership. I brought in someone with real systems and real relationships. We closed the rest in 30 days.

That deal taught me something crucial:
Capital doesn't move on urgency. It moves on confidence.
And confidence comes from clarity.

Why Investors Really Say "No"

It's not always the deal. It's the discomfort.

Most of your investors aren't professional LPs. They're doctors, lawyers, business owners, and high performers in other industries. They're smart—but not always confident when it comes to syndication structures, tax terms, or waterfalls.

They say no not because they dislike you.
They say no because they don't want to feel stupid—or get burned.

If someone doesn't understand IRR or a preferred return, they won't ask. They'll just walk away.

▶ **Red Flag: Confused Investors Are Quiet Until They Panic**
If you don't educate them upfront, they'll nod during the pitch, invest anyway, and then freak out when distributions fluctuate or delays happen. Now you're managing fear—not capital.
Clarity is the cure.

The Shift: From Pitchman to Partner

After that $3M deal, I stopped trying to close investors. Instead, I started equipping them.

Now, education comes first—long before the raise begins. We break things down:

- What "preferred return" really means
- How waterfalls work—and when they don't
- What the capital stack is, and where LPs actually sit
- Why tax advantages are powerful—but not a guarantee

By the time we open a deal, the raise moves faster—not because we push harder, but because we've already answered the objections before they're asked.

If you remove confusion, you remove resistance.

Capital Raising Red Flags

Here's what makes me walk away from a raise—or a sponsor running one:

▶ **Too Much Sizzle, Not Enough Substance**
If a raise is full of steak dinners, first-class flights, or flash without fundamentals, I ask: Where's that money coming from? Probably your check.

▶ **Heavy Pressure Tactics**
If you're told "you'll miss out" or "this will fill in 24 hours," be cautious. Great deals get filled—but they don't need to be forced.

▶ **No Real Infrastructure**
If a sponsor is using Excel to manage millions, that's a red flag. What else are they managing by hand?

▶ Unverifiable Track Record
You should be able to ask: "What were the last three deals? What were the projections vs. actuals? Who can I talk to?" If you can't verify it, don't wire into it.

▶ No Clear Risk Disclosure
If the deal pitch skips the downside scenarios or feels like pure optimism, the risk isn't being managed—it's being ignored.

▶ Red Flag: Social Media Charisma Without Operational Clarity

Some sponsors have a strong online presence—and that's not inherently a bad thing. In fact, it can be a green flag. The best operators often share deal updates, lessons learned, and transparent breakdowns of what's working (and what's not).

But there's a fine line between building trust and building a personal brand.

If a sponsor is constantly online—but it's all lifestyle photos, vague buzzwords, and ego-driven flexing—you have to ask:

What's behind the curtain?
Flashy content without operational substance is a red flag. So is silence when deals underperform. If the only thing being marketed is the sponsor—and not the deal fundamentals—your risk is higher than it looks.

Before you wire funds, scroll their feed and ask:

- Do they share real data—or just dopamine hits?
- Are they open about challenges—or only highlight wins?
- Do they show the team and process—or just the lifestyle?

Charisma can raise capital. But character and execution return it.

The Excel Problem: Financials That Can't Be Trusted

When you're raising capital, trust begins with transparency.

Sponsors ask sellers for financials before buying a property. Investors should do the same before funding a deal.

If your sponsor can't—or won't—provide:

- Clean profit & loss statements
- Rent rolls
- Operating budgets
- Property performance to date

That's not a partnership. That's a blind date with your capital.

▶ **Red Flag: Financials only exist in Excel**
Why that's a problem:

1. **Lack of controls** – Excel doesn't track changes or lock data. Numbers can be tweaked without a trace.
2. **No audit trail** – You can't see version history or who changed what.
3. **Manual errors** – One wrong cell = millions in miscalculation.

Professional operators use Yardi, AppFolio, or Buildium. If you're sending six figures and they're tracking rent on a spreadsheet, that's a problem.

Final Word: Education Is the Raise

Your investors don't need to become underwriters. They just need to feel safe, seen, and smart.

When you educate:

- You lower the fear threshold
- You build conviction

- You attract better-fit capital

And most importantly?
You earn the kind of trust that lasts longer than a single deal.

The next chapter will dive into how different asset classes carry different risks—and how to spot the red flags unique to each one. Because real capital alignment isn't just about raising money.
It's about **raising the right expectations**.

CHAPTER 11
UNDERSTANDING ASSET CLASSES—WHAT YOU'RE ACTUALLY INVESTING IN

Not all syndications are created equal. And not all risk shows up in the pitch deck.

One of the biggest mistakes passive investors make is assuming that real estate is real estate. As if an apartment building, a RV park, and a storage facility all operate the same way. They don't.

The asset class behind the deal plays a massive role in shaping the returns, the tax profile, the risk level, and the timeline of your investment. It determines:

- How volatile the income might be
- How specialized the operator needs to be
- How exposed you are when the market shifts

A great sponsor can make a difficult asset work. A bad one can destroy even the safest deal. But either way, you need to know what you're buying into.

Because every asset class has **unique red flags**—especially the ones nobody talks about.

This chapter breaks down the most common asset types in syndications. You'll see how they work, where the returns come from, where deals go wrong, and how to decide whether that asset belongs in *your* portfolio. This chapter isn't about ranking asset classes.

The only one I recommend timing carefully is oil & gas. Not because it's bad, but because it carries unique risks and tax considerations that make it better suited for later in your investment journey.

1. Multifamily (Apartments)

Why It Works:

- Constant housing demand = stable occupancy
- Renovation/upside potential through value-add strategies
- Reasonable financing terms, especially from agency lenders

Multifamily is the bread and butter of many syndicators—and for good reason. When done well, it offers a predictable path to cash flow and appreciation. Renovations increase rents, bump NOI, and create forced appreciation.

But many sponsors oversimplify the playbook. They assume what worked in 2019 will work today. It won't.

Red Flags to Watch For:

- ⚑ Rent bump assumptions without verified comps
- ⚑ CapEx budgets that don't match the scope of work
- ⚑ Overly optimistic timelines for lease-up or renovations
- ⚑ Luxury/Class A projects in overbuilt markets
- ⚑ A parking lot full of cars at 10am (who's actually working?)
- ⚑ A busy sales history, example 3 owners in 5 years
- ⚑ "Occupied" units with no belongings, no signs of life, and no real tenant

- ▶ Collections that look solid—until you realize they're choppy and unreliable
- ▶ Multiple expired leases or leases that don't match the rent roll
- ▶ Signs of deferred maintenance, such as stained ceilings, peeling paint, or cracks in walls
- ▶ Purchasing at or above replacement cost
- ▶ No mention of property management or tenant profile
- ▶ Not stress testing the pro forma
- ▶ Final debt terms not clear

Real Example: I saw a deck once that showed a projected 30% rent increase in 12 months with "minor renovations." When I checked the comps, they were in a different school district and had pools, gyms, and dog parks. The deal fell apart before closing.

Smart LP Questions:

- "What's your average unit turnover cost?"
- "What happens if rents only rise 2%, not 6%?"
- "Who's managing the property—and have they managed in this submarket?"

Multifamily can be dependable—if managed well. But it's still vulnerable to aggressive underwriting and operational missteps. Some red flags apply to the sponsor, but if you're investing alongside them, they apply to you too. For a deeper checklist, just reach out.

2. Mobile Home Parks

Why It Works:

- Sticky tenants = low turnover
- Strong demand for affordable housing
- Often own the land, not the homes = fewer headaches

MHPs are one of the most misunderstood asset classes. People picture rundown trailers and mismanagement. But well-run parks offer stable income, low expenses, and minimal capital expenditures.

The problem? Many investors (and sponsors) underestimate the infrastructure risks.

Red Flags to Watch For:

- 🚩 Private utilities (well/septic) with no upgrade plan
- 🚩 Unclear zoning or use-rights
- 🚩 Collections that look solid—until you realize they're choppy and unreliable
- 🚩 No reserves for roads or underground infrastructure
- 🚩 Relying on tenant-owned homes without enforcing upkeep
- 🚩 High number of park-owned homes requiring repairs
- 🚩 Unclear ownership records or ongoing legal disputes

LP Pitfall: Just because tenants own their homes doesn't mean they maintain them. And if 20% of the park turns into vacant pads with derelict trailers, your income drops and your park starts to decay.

Smart LP Questions:

- "How many lots use city water and sewer?"
- "What's the average pad rent vs. market?"
- "Are there abandoned units or empty pads—and what's the plan for them?"

MHPs are resilient—but only if the bones are solid. Think utilities, roads, and zoning. One red flag? Collections. Depending on the tenant base, they can be a recurring issue in this asset class.

3. RV Parks

Why It Works:

- Flexible pricing models (daily, weekly, monthly)
- Strong cash flow potential in the right markets
- Alternative affordable housing in some regions

RV parks are a blend of hospitality and housing. That's part of the opportunity—and the danger. They can outperform when tourism is strong, but they're labor-intensive and highly seasonal.

Red Flags to Watch For:

- ⚑ Modeling year-round occupancy in seasonal areas
- ⚑ Sponsors with no hospitality or transient experience
- ⚑ No onsite manager or systems for turnover
- ⚑ No plan for dealing with bad online reviews

LP Pitfall: One investor told me about a park that operated at 80% occupancy—until it got three one-star Google reviews due to water outages and no staff. Within 60 days, occupancy dropped to 30%.

Smart LP Questions:

- "What's the breakdown of seasonal vs. long-term tenants?"
- "How is guest experience managed and reviewed?"
- "Do you have professional reservation and review systems in place?"

RV parks can be very profitable—but only if treated like a business, not a campground.

4. Industrial (Warehouses, Flex Space)

Why It Works:

- **Long Leases + Credit Tenants = Predictable Income**
  Industrial leases often span 5–15 years, with annual escalations. When your tenant is Amazon or FedEx, that's dependable cash flow.
- **Tailwinds: E-Commerce and Reshoring**
  E-commerce and reshoring trends are fueling demand. Online shopping, same-day delivery, and U.S. manufacturing trends are fueling relentless demand for logistics space.
- **Low Turnover, Low Operating Costs**
  These aren't high-maintenance buildings. No elevators, no HVAC for common areas, no fussy tenants. Operating margins can be impressive.
- **Tenant Quality**
  Industrial tends to attract institutional-grade tenants—Fortune 500s, government contractors, and logistics giants.

Industrial is the new darling of CRE. And while the fundamentals are strong, it's not a simple asset class. Single-tenant deals are deceptively risky. And highly specialized buildouts (like cold storage or clean rooms) reduce your flexibility.

Red Flags to Watch For:

- ▶ Single-tenant dependency
- ▶ No fallback plan if the tenant vacates
- ▶ Specialized buildouts with limited secondary uses
- ▶ Lack of verification on tenant creditworthiness

Real Case: One sponsor acquired a warehouse leased to a cannabis company. Looked great—until cannabis was reclassified as high-risk by their lender. Refi terms vanished. So did the tenant.

Smart LP Questions:

- "What's the tenant's credit and lease history?"
- "If the tenant leaves, who else would lease this space?"
- "What are the lease terms—can the tenant terminate early?"

Industrial works best when the leases are long and the buildings are versatile with tenants that are wealthier than we are.

5. Self-Storage

Why It Works:

- Driven by life events: death, divorce, downsizing
- Low management and op-ex
- Short-term leases = pricing agility

Self-storage seems simple—but competition has exploded. Oversupply, bad tenants, and weak digital presence can erode margins fast. And sellers? Many don't keep clean books.

Red Flags to Watch For:

- ▶ Market saturation (too many new units chasing limited demand)
- ▶ Underperforming facility with no clear reason why
- ▶ High delinquencies or accounts receivable over 10%
- ▶ Poor tenant quality (frequent damage, payment issues, misuse)
- ▶ Seller can't provide tax returns, rent rolls, or clean P&Ls
- ▶ Outdated pricing strategy or lack of digital marketing
- ▶ Deferred maintenance or site safety concerns
- ▶ Environmental risks (e.g. floodplain, contamination)
- ▶ Overreliance on "physical" occupancy vs. true paying tenants

Pro Tip:
Look at the gap between physical and **economic** occupancy. 90% full sounds great—until you learn 40% of those tenants aren't paying.

Smart LP Questions:

- "What's your Google review rating?"
- "What's the digital marketing budget?"
- "Are collections handled in-house or outsourced?"
- "What's your average days delinquent and A/R ratio?"

Storage is great—if it's run like an online business with a physical storefront. It's recession-resilient and can deliver strong returns. **Biggest threats? Oversupply and lazy management.**

6. Office Buildings

Why It Works:

- Long leases with stable tenants
- Triple-net structures shift cost burdens to tenants

Office is no longer a generalist asset class. It's a surgical one. If you don't understand the tenant base, leasing trends, and Class A vs. Class B/B- dynamics, it's easy to misread the risk.

Red Flags to Watch For:

- ▶ Vacancy in remote-work-heavy cities (SF, DC, Seattle)
- ▶ No repositioning budget for dated space
- ▶ Short lease roll with no tenant renewal discussions
- ▶ Outdated HVAC and security systems

LP Pitfall: Office looks appealing because the leases are long. But, if 70% of the rent roll expires in Year 3, that "stability" is a mirage.

7. Retail

Why It Works:

- Triple-net leases = low overhead
- Service-based and grocery-anchored centers perform well

Retail isn't dead—but e-commerce and changing foot traffic patterns have killed off a lot of subtypes.

Red Flags to Watch For:

- ▶ High lease rollover without visibility into renewals
- ▶ Anchors that are nonessential (fitness, fashion)
- ▶ Poor ingress/egress or visibility
- ▶ High Market Vacancy
- ▶ Declining Population

Smart LP Questions:

- "How much of the rent roll expires in the next 2 years?"
- "What percentage of tenants are local vs. national?"
- "How is the center marketed to the community?"

Retail can be resilient—but the strategy needs to reflect 2025, not 2005.

8. Distressed Debt & Recap Funds

Why It Works:

- Buy at a discount, solve a problem, unlock value
- Often uncorrelated with public markets

Distressed debt funds sound sexy—but they require immense operational skill. You're not just buying paper. You're stepping into broken systems and trying to fix them.

Red Flags to Watch For:

- ▶ Sponsor has never worked out a distressed deal
- ▶ Legal strategy is vague or reliant on fast foreclosure
- ▶ Timelines are overly optimistic
- ▶ Exit is based on "the market coming back"

These are chess matches, not checkers. Only invest if you trust the strategist and know what you are buying. Some of these funds are just repackaged cash calls—real estate's version of junk bonds.

9. Oil & Gas Syndications

Why It Works:

- Massive first-year tax benefits (IDC deductions)
- Uncorrelated with real estate and equity markets
- Huge upside on successful wells

Red Flags to Watch For:

- ▶ No third-party engineering or reserve reports
- ▶ No clear control of the well or operator transparency
- ▶ Cash flow projections without decline curve modeling
- ▶ Guarantees, claims they never hit a dry hole

Oil and gas syndications can be powerful—but they should be the last rung on the ladder, not the first. Personally, I believe in owning stocks, real estate, and gold before even considering oil and gas.

Here's why: **the risk.**

Think about it—major players like ExxonMobil aren't raising capital from retail investors. In fact, they haven't issued new shares since a 2-for-1 stock split in 2001. And when they needed liquidity during the COVID crash in 2020, they issued **debt**, not equity.

Translation? They don't need your money.

So when I see operators who've raised $500 million or more still soliciting retail funds, I have to ask: *Why?*

If their GP promote is 30%, and the deals are supposedly offering a two-year payback, shouldn't they already be swimming in cash? Thirty percent of $500 million is $150 million—that's $75 million a year.

To be fair, there is one legitimate reason they might continue raising capital: to spread risk across investors, just like in real estate. But real estate is far less liquid and often pays out at the end of a five-year hold. In oil and gas, the payout timelines and volatility are very different. You need to be crystal clear on the risks you're sharing.

Just make sure you're comfortable with the exposure **before** you jump in.

Here's the bottom line:
Exxon isn't pitching investors on LinkedIn.

So in this space, I'm often more inclined to back a smaller, proven operator—someone nimble, transparent, and honest about their scope—rather than a flashy fund claiming to have raised $500 million to $1 billion and still passing the hat.

If they've truly had that level of success, and they're not buying massive assets directly from the majors, why do they still need your money?

LP Rule: Don't go looking for oil until you've built a financial house that can withstand dry holes.

▶ Big red flag? An operator who claims they've never hit a dry hole or offers guarantees. That's not confidence. That's a con. Even Exxon has dry holes in their SEC filings.

I like this asset class—but only if you're financially and mentally ready. Smart operators know how to manage risk—through royalties, reworks, diversification, or existing production. If you're looking at a deal and want a second opinion, feel free to reach out.

10. Senior Living

Why It Works:

- Aging demographics = built-in demand
- Recession-resilient need for housing and care
- Potential for hybrid income models (rent + care services)

Senior housing is one of the fastest-growing asset classes in real estate, but it's also one of the most operationally intense. It's not just a building—it's a healthcare-adjacent business. Memory care, assisted living, and independent living all have different needs, staffing models, and compliance requirements.

Red Flags to Watch For:

- ▶ No prior healthcare or senior housing experience
- ▶ Underestimating staffing costs or turnover
- ▶ Overreliance on private pay in markets with low median income
- ▶ No contingency for regulatory changes or liability insurance

Smart LP Questions:

- "What's your staff-to-resident ratio?"
- "What licenses are required in this state, and who holds them?"
- "How do you handle turnover in caregiving staff?"

A missed payroll in multifamily causes inconvenience. In senior housing, it causes lawsuits. This isn't an asset class for amateurs.

11. Data Centers

Why It Works:

- Explosive demand from AI, cloud storage, and content delivery
- Long-term leases with sticky tenants (tech firms, hyperscalers)
- High barriers to entry

Data centers are infrastructure plays in disguise. These buildings power the modern digital economy—but they're also power-hungry, capital-intensive, and highly technical.

Red Flags to Watch For:

- ▶ Inadequate power, cooling, or fiber connectivity
- ▶ High upfront or recurring capex not built into projections
- ▶ Obsolete tech infrastructure in a fast-evolving environment
- ▶ Tenant concentration risk—especially with hyperscalers
- ▶ Weak cybersecurity or unclear server ownership structure
- ▶ Regulatory exposure (data laws, geopolitical risks)

Smart LP Questions:

- "How many kilowatts per cabinet does the facility support?"
- "What's the backup power system—and how often is it tested?"
- "Is the tenant managing their own racks, or is the sponsor providing services?"

Data centers can produce cash like industrial—but they operate more like hospitals. Mission-critical uptime = mission-critical operations.

12. Cold Storage

Why It Works:

- High demand from food logistics, pharmaceuticals, and e-commerce
- Limited supply = pricing power
- Recession-resistant fundamentals

Cold storage is industrial real estate on steroids. Temperatures range from +40°F to -10°F—and missing those targets isn't just a tenant complaint. It's a lawsuit. That risk is why leases tend to be long and sticky.

Red Flags to Watch For:

- ▶ No experience with temperature-controlled assets
- ▶ Energy inefficiency or outdated cooling infrastructure (Freon phase-outs, undersized systems)
- ▶ Low ceilings (<24 ft), too few dock doors, or poor loading flow
- ▶ Misalignment between freezer/cooler/ambient mix and tenant needs
- ▶ No rail access in a market where it's expected
- ▶ Office space that's too large (or too small) for operational demands
- ▶ Failure to account for higher maintenance capex—especially on aging systems

Smart LP Questions:

- "What percentage of the space is freezer vs. cooler vs. ambient?"
- "Is the facility using ammonia or Freon—and are systems up to code?"
- "How is energy usage monitored and optimized?"
- "Are reserves adjusted for cold-chain wear and tear?"

Cold storage leases can stretch 15+ years, but one mechanical failure can end the relationship overnight.

13. Build-to-Rent (BTR) Communities

Definition:
Build-to-Rent refers to purpose-built residential communities of single-family homes or townhomes constructed specifically as rentals—not for sale to individual homeowners.

Why Investors Like It:
BTR combines the stability and tenant quality of single-family rentals with the scale and operational efficiency of multifamily. With rising home prices and tighter mortgage access, many families are choosing to rent longer—yet still want the privacy of a home.

Common Structures:

- Often structured as syndications or institutional joint ventures
- Leases tend to be longer-term than apartments
- Professionally managed with shared amenities (e.g., pool, clubhouse, lawn care)

Attractive Traits:

- High retention: Families renting homes often stay longer than apartment renters
- Strong demand tailwinds: Younger families priced out of homeownership
- Operational efficiency: Centralized management over many similar units
- Exit optionality: Can be sold as a portfolio or as individual units for retail sale

Red Flags to Watch:

- ▶ Overbuilding in the same submarket—especially if multiple BTR projects are chasing the same tenant pool
- ▶ Underwritten using outdated rent growth or cap rate assumptions
- ▶ Delayed lease-up and cash flow due to high upfront development costs
- ▶ Construction shortcuts to meet scale—leads to future maintenance headaches
- ▶ High accounts receivable or tenant turnover despite "new build" status
- ▶ Zoning restrictions, community pushback, or HOA conflicts over rentals
- ▶ Sponsor inexperience with managing horizontal multifamily (vs. vertical apartments)
- ▶ Exit plans that rely on cap rate compression or speculative individual home sales
- ▶ Unclear delineation between builder, operator, and asset manager
- ▶ Rising management and maintenance costs tied to shared amenities
- ▶ Limited historical performance data—especially in non-core markets

LP Tip:
Ask whether the builder and the operator are the same entity—or if the sponsor has a proven track record managing scattered-site rentals. Building homes is one business. Operating rentals at scale is another.

Example:
A 120-home BTR community in Phoenix leases to families earning $80K–$120K per year. Renters enjoy private yards, garages, and shared amenities. Sponsor plans to hold for 7 years, then exit via bulk portfolio sale or retail disposition.

📖 Deep Dive: RV Parks and Seasonality

Previously, we covered RV parks' operational complexity and exposure to reviews. Let's go one layer deeper.

The real risk in RV parks isn't just seasonality—it's *mispricing seasonality*.

If your underwriting assumes July revenue in December, you've got a problem. Many parks are highly dependent on peak season—Memorial Day to Labor Day—and crash hard outside that window.

Also: RV parks in snowbird states (AZ, FL, NM, TX) often rely on a *migratory customer base*. If fuel costs spike or retirement incomes drop, occupancy tanks.

More Red Flags to Watch For:

- ▶ Pro forma doesn't adjust for off-season vacancy
- ▶ No segmented P&L for peak vs. shoulder vs. off-season months
- ▶ Park lacks appeal to both full-timers and weekenders
- ▶ Zero margin built in for weather events (e.g. wildfires, flooding, hurricanes)

Advanced LP Questions:

- "What % of revenue is earned in the top 3 months?"
- "How have off-season rates been adjusted historically?"
- "Is there a long-term tenant base that stabilizes income?"

RV parks aren't just housing—they're part tourism, part customer service, and part weather risk. If the operator doesn't get that, the whole deal can go off the rails.

With that being said, RV parks can be one of the best asset classes— and one of my personal favorites—when done right. When the location, management, and systems align, they can offer powerful cash flow, low overhead, and high demand in markets that hotels and apartments can't touch. But it only works if the sponsor treats it like a business, not a campground.

I'm drawn to RV parks with minimal amenities and lower overhead—no pool, no resort-style frills. They tend to attract longer-term tenants, carry fewer insurance and maintenance costs, and are most attractive when located near steady employment and economic activity.

> 🔁 **Deep Dive: Commercial construction is one of the most powerful ways to build generational wealth — yet it's also one of the riskiest if you don't know what danger looks like before it strikes.**

Ask any seasoned developer or investor, and they'll tell you: most problems don't appear overnight. They start as small cracks — subtle red flags that, if ignored, grow into budget overruns, endless delays, lawsuits, or failed assets that never reach their full potential.

This chapter is your early-warning radar: a concise but powerful guide to the *real-world red flags* that quietly wreck projects. And more importantly, it's a reminder that the strongest defense for your capital is selecting a general contractor who can spot these pitfalls for you — and handle them before they become catastrophic.

Ten Red Flags That Should Make You Hit Pause

Over the years, these are the warning signs I've seen sink even the best-looking projects. Learn them. Watch for them. Act decisively when they appear.

1.) Vague or Incomplete Scope of Work

If the scope is fuzzy, so is your budget. Gaps in plans, half-finished specs, or generic "to be determined" allowances all but guarantee expensive change orders and miscommunication down the line. A detailed scope is your anchor — without it, the project drifts.

2.) Too-Good-to-Be-True Lowball Bids

A bid that comes in dramatically lower than everyone else's is a flashing red light. Some contractors undercut the competition to win the work, fully intending to recover losses through inflated change orders or substandard materials. If it feels too good to be true, trust your gut — it is.

3.) Unproven or Unstable Contractor

No matter how polished the pitch, you need to see verifiable experience, relevant references, and financial stability. A contractor with a trail of lawsuits, unpaid subs, or bankruptcies in their past may become your problem next.

4.) Payment Delays to Subcontractors

When subcontractors and suppliers aren't paid on time, they walk — or file liens that can tie up your property in legal knots. Ask around: if you hear grumblings of late payments, investigate. A well-run project pays its people — period.

5.) Early Schedule Slippage

Delays in the first stages — sitework, foundations, or utilities — rarely fix themselves. Instead, they compound. If a project is off track before vertical construction begins, expect to pay a premium in overtime or accept that the delivery date may slip by months.

6.) Permitting Problems or Unsafe Site Practices

Missing permits or a lax safety culture is a deal breaker. A single stop-work order can freeze your timeline for weeks — while accidents on site open you up to insurance claims, fines, or worse. Safety isn't just about compliance; it's a sign of operational discipline.

7.) Revolving Door of Project Staff

A strong contractor keeps a consistent, capable team. Frequent turnover — especially for your project manager or superintendent — destroys continuity, knowledge transfer, and accountability. Watch for signs that key people keep disappearing.

8.) No Quality Control Process

A legitimate builder can show you their punch list process, inspection milestones, and how they handle rework. If they can't explain it, expect callbacks, warranty claims, and dissatisfied tenants down the road.

9.) Unrealistic Timelines

Aggressive schedules can win the bid but rarely work in the real world. When a GC promises the moon with no reasonable basis, you're the one who pays for the overtime, premium labor, and stress to finish.

10.) Lack of Clear Communication

Silence kills projects. A GC who can't communicate clearly — through regular updates, transparent reporting, and proactive problem-solving — is guaranteed to let problems fester until they're too costly to fix.

Why a Quality General Contractor is Your Best Insurance Policy

Here's the part too many passive investors underestimate once the ink dries, you're not building that project — your GC is. You can have the best architect, an airtight lease, and eager tenants lined up. But if your contractor can't deliver, everything else falls apart.

A truly capable general contractor does more than pour concrete and swing hammers:

- They **protect your budget** by coordinating trades, managing subs, and catching costly issues before they escalate.
- They **guard your schedule**, so your rent roll starts when your pro forma says it should.
- They **uphold safety and compliance**, shielding you from lawsuits, fines, and reputational damage.
- They **deliver quality that lasts**, preserving the long-term value and operating efficiency of your asset.
- And they **communicate openly**, ensuring you're never left in the dark about risks or solutions.

In passive investments or joint ventures, your GC is your eyes, ears, and boots on the ground. They're the single biggest factor in whether your project becomes an income-generating cornerstone or an expensive cautionary tale. Ryzec Building Group, LLC exemplifies what it means to deliver high-quality construction for retail, quick-service restaurant (QSR), and car wash developments — making them a trusted partner for investors seeking dependable, passive income-generating assets.

Protect Your Capital, Protect Your Peace of Mind

Spotting red flags isn't about paranoia — it's about preparation. The best investors don't just throw money at drawings and hope for the best. They build teams of seasoned professionals, insist on transparency, and partner with contractors who treat every dollar like it's their own.

A good general contractor won't shy away from this level of accountability — they'll welcome it. They know their reputation depends on your success. So, trust your gut, do your homework, and don't settle for anything less than a partner who can prove they have your back.

Because in commercial construction, small cracks become sinkholes fast. Spot the signs, act early, and your project — and your portfolio — will thank you for years to come.

Final words from Nick Johnson:
Build wisely. Invest carefully. And always, always choose your partners well.

You can reach Nick directly at:
Nick.xj.johnson@gmail.com
615.332.2369

Final Word: Asset Classes Aren't Good or Bad—But Sponsors Can Be

There's no one-size-fits-all winner in investing.

Every asset class has its strengths—and its risks. The real question is whether the sponsor truly understands what they're operating and whether they're being transparent about the downside.

The best LPs don't chase hype.
They back operators with discipline, track records, and a deep understanding of the asset.
They know a great deal doesn't hide from scrutiny—it welcomes it.

So don't just ask, *"What's the return?"*

Ask, *"What could go wrong—and who's driving the bus if it does?"*

Because here's the truth:
Every asset class has potential. But that doesn't mean *you* are ready for every asset class.

▶ One of the biggest red flags?
Jumping into something you aren't financially or emotionally equipped to handle.
Leaning on experts is smart.
Blindly diving in? That's dangerous.

I didn't start in commercial real estate. I didn't buy gold before I had cash flow and I definitely didn't drill for oil until I built a foundation.

Like most investors, I started small: First stocks, then real estate, then gold, then oil came last.

Over time, I earned the right to take bigger swings—because I became a better investor.
More disciplined, more informed, and more prepared.

People ask me about oil & gas a lot.
It's a powerful asset class—but probably the *last* one you should own.

Not because it's bad, because it's risky.
And risk should be earned, not assumed.

PART V
THINKING LIKE A WEALTH BUILDER

CHAPTER 12
HOW ECONOMIC CONDITIONS REVEAL RED FLAGS

What Happens When the Market Shifts—and the Operator Doesn't

Most investors don't lose money because they picked the wrong property.

They lose money because they backed the wrong assumptions.

You can buy a great building in a strong market and still lose if the operator is in denial about rising rates, supply gluts, or shifting tenant behavior.

A sponsor betting on interest rates dropping next quarter... while the Fed is still hiking?
⚑ That's a red flag.

A syndicator assuming 7% rent growth in a market with stagnant job growth and falling absorption?
⚑ Another red flag.

You don't need to be an economist to invest successfully.
But you do need to understand how the economic environment exposes weakness—in strategies, in assumptions, and in the people running the deals.

1. Why the Macro Picture Matters

Real estate isn't immune to the broader economy. It's built on top of it.

Syndications live or die by macro trends—whether the sponsor admits it or not. Macro forces shape everything:

- Interest rates dictate debt terms and cap rates
- Inflation drives costs and rent potential
- Employment affects leasing, renewals, and retail traffic
- Consumer confidence shapes tenant behavior
- Market cycles determine what kind of risk gets rewarded—or punished

▶ **Red Flag: Sponsors who ignore the economic backdrop—or worse, bet against it.**
One of the most dangerous patterns in this industry? Assuming the future will look like the past.
That's not underwriting. That's wishful thinking.

2. Economic Levers That Move the Needle

Interest Rates

If you only pay attention to one macro factor as an LP, make it this one.

Higher interest rates impact:

- Loan payments (higher monthly obligations = lower cash flow)
- Property values (as cap rates rise, values fall)
- Exit assumptions (who's buying, and at what yield?)

Yet many sponsors keep underwriting deals at cap rates that assume rates will fall next year.

🚩 **Red Flag: Underwriting the future based on a Powell pivot that hasn't happened.**

Smart LP Filters:

- Look for fixed-rate debt or at least rate caps
- Ask to see a sensitivity table (What happens if rates stay flat or rise?)
- If they can't show the IRR with conservative rates—it's not a real deal. It's a bet.

Inflation

Inflation is a double-edged sword. It's not always bad—but it's never neutral.

On one hand:

- Short-term leases (multifamily, storage, mobile homes) can reprice quickly
- Property values may rise with replacement costs

But on the other hand:

- Expenses balloon (especially insurance, payroll, and materials)
- Tenants feel squeezed—and churn increases
- Lenders tighten, making refis harder and slower

🚩 **Red Flag: Assuming rent growth will always outpace expense growth.**
In 2022–2023, many sponsors modeled 5%–7% rent growth—but ignored that insurance premiums were doubling in states like Texas and Florida.
Result? Flat or declining NOI despite rising gross income.

Smart LP Filters:

- Ask to see both gross and net income projections
- Request historical op-ex ratios for the same market
- Ask what inflation assumptions were used for expenses

Employment & Consumer Confidence

Real estate doesn't work without tenants. Tenants don't pay without jobs. Retail, multifamily, even industrial—all suffer when unemployment rises or sentiment drops.

▶ **Red Flag: "It's always been strong here" used as a replacement for actual market research.**

Smart LP Filters:

- Ask for local employment concentration data
- Look for job diversity: tech-only markets are brittle
- Ask what percentage of tenants are renewing vs. turning over

Example: A deal in San Francisco looked solid... until 30% of tenants worked for tech firms that implemented hybrid work. Occupancy didn't drop—but renewals did. It took 14 months to stabilize.

3. The Real Estate Cycle: Where Are We Now?

Understanding where we are in the market cycle isn't about calling tops and bottoms. It's about knowing what types of risk are being rewarded—or punished.

Every cycle has four stages:

● *Expansion*

- Rising demand

- Rent growth
- New construction
- Confidence everywhere
  ▶ **Red Flag: Overpaying in a frenzy.** Everyone's buying. Few are underwriting with discipline.

Peak

- Prices top out
- Rent growth slows
- Interest rates start rising
  ▶ **Red Flag: Chasing deals just to deploy capital.** Watch for short-term holds, slim margins, or "creative" exits.

Recession

- Vacancies rise
- Rent growth turns negative
- Foreclosures increase
- Buyers disappear
  ▶ **Red Flag: Sponsors stretched too thin.** Watch for bridge debt, floating rates, or syndicators trying to "save" deals with capital calls.

Recovery

- Demand returns slowly
- Value-add starts working again
- Smart sponsors reposition and buy at discounts
  ▶ **Red Flag: Operators sitting on bad assets with no plan.** Inaction is often fatal during recovery.

4. How to Match Strategy to the Moment

Good sponsors adjust their playbook based on the cycle.

Here's what that looks like:

Expansion Playbook:

- Take calculated risk
- Value-add and repositioning deals make sense
- Cap rate compression may help, but don't rely on it

Peak Playbook:

- Focus on cash flow and durability
- Avoid heavy CapEx or big turnaround bets
- Lock in long-term fixed debt

Recession Playbook:

- Be patient—but ready
- Have dry powder
- Look at distressed debt or recap funds if you know the operator is skilled

Recovery Playbook:

- Underwrite stability, not speed
- Renovation and lease-up deals work—but only with real comps

5. What LPs Should Be Watching (Right Now)

You don't need to call the cycle. But you do need to see if the deal is fighting the cycle—or riding it.

☑ **Does the sponsor's strategy fit the cycle?**

Ask:

- Are they using fixed-rate or hedged debt?

- Are they buying in a market with job growth—or just one that used to be hot?
- Are their assumptions based on 2021 thinking—or 2025 realities?

☑ **Are they operating with margin?**
Deals today need buffers, reserve accounts, conservative rent growth, realistic expense modeling.
▶ Red Flag: Thin underwriting that only works in Goldilocks conditions.

☑ **Do they understand the timeline?**
Real estate is not a **Sprint**. Sponsors promising 24-month flips in a tightening market are gambling.
▶ Red Flag: Talking more about exit caps than business execution.

☑ **Are they thinking like builders—or traders?**
One of the clearest economic red flags isn't in the model. It's in the mindset. Sponsors who chase IRR over durability, who obsess over short-term exits, or who rely on appreciation over NOI—those are speculators, not operators.
▶ Red Flag: "We'll sell in two years and 1031 into something better."

Ask:

- "What if the market's soft in 24 months?"
- "What's the plan if rates stay flat?"
- "Have you operated through a down cycle?"

6. How the Best Sponsors React to Economic Shifts

When the market shifts, weak sponsors hope and strong sponsors adapt.

The Best Sponsors:

- Pause acquisitions when pricing disconnects from fundamentals

- Reprice deals that no longer make sense
- Shift business plans: reduce CapEx, lengthen holds, reposition marketing
- Communicate proactively, even when news is bad

The Weakest Sponsors:

- Push forward to "prove" they can still win
- Rely on outdated comparables
- Double down on marketing instead of management
- Go silent when distributions miss

7. Case Study: 2022–2023

The Deal:
A value-add multifamily in Phoenix, was underwritten in 2021 with a 5-year hold, and a projected 18% IRR. That has a floating rate debt with a rate cap.

What Happened:

- Interest rates jumped 500 bps
- Insurance and labor costs spiked
- Rent growth stalled at 2%
- Refinance in Year 3 became impossible
- Distributions paused

Where Red Flags Were Missed:

- No fixed debt = exposure to rate hikes
- Sponsor assumed 5% rent growth every year
- No budget for cost inflation or extended hold
- No downside sensitivity modeling shared with LPs

This wasn't a terrible property.

It was a **misread** market + **unrealistic** model = ▶ red flags that were visible to any LP asking hard questions.

Final Word: The Market Reveals the Truth

Economic conditions don't cause weak deals.
They expose them.

They expose:

- Thin underwriting
- Hope-based assumptions
- Sponsor inexperience
- Lack of adaptability

The best passive investors aren't trying to be macro wizards; they're just listening for mismatches.

If the sponsor's assumptions feel outdated...
If the model only works if the Fed pivots...
If the communication breaks down when the winds change...
That's your signal.

When the cycle shifts, you don't want a hype artist. You want a steward.

The best deals aren't built for ideal conditions.
They're built to survive change.

So the next time a sponsor sends a pitch, ask yourself:
"Does this deal know what year it is?"
If not?
▶ That's your red flag.

Family office event in Miami, focused on diligence and deal structuring.

CHAPTER 13
FROM SCARCITY TO STRATEGY— REWIRING THE RED FLAGS IN YOUR MONEY MINDSET

We grow up believing control equals safety.
That if we can just hold on tight enough—our job, our money, our time—we'll be okay.

It makes sense. Control feels safe.
But when it comes to wealth building, that mindset can be a red flag in disguise.

Because the need for control often masks something deeper: **FEAR.**

▶ **The Illusion of Control**

If you're a high achiever, you probably got here by taking charge.
You built your business. You made the calls. You controlled outcomes.

So when it comes to investing, letting go feels like a risk.
Trusting a sponsor?
Riding out a dip instead of selling?
Letting a system work without micromanaging it?

That feels vulnerable.

But it's not gambling—it's strategy.

The red flag here?
Mistaking control for security.

Control isn't what keeps you safe **Process** is.
Conviction is.
Systems are.

Warren Buffett said it best:

"Our favorite holding period is forever."

He wasn't just talking stocks—he was talking about mindset.

Managing Risk vs. Avoiding It

Scarcity mindset says:

"Don't take risks."

Strategic mindset says:

"Understand your risks—and plan for them."

Every investor faces risk.
But the confident ones do it with buffers, clarity, and a plan.
They don't chase certainty—they manage uncertainty.

▶ **Red Flag Behavior:**

- Hoarding cash "just in case"
- Panicking in a downturn
- Pulling out of a deal because of a headline
- Jumping into something because it feels "Safe" without running the numbers

None of that is strategy.
It's fear in disguise.

🧠 The Confident Investor Framework

How to Train Your Brain for Strategic Investing

1. **Know Your Goals**
   → What are you really solving for—freedom, cash flow, legacy?
   → Goals eliminate guesswork. They're your North Star.
2. **Define Your Filters**
   → What deals, operators, and markets are a yes—or a hard no?
   → Your red flag list should be written in ink.
3. **Build a Repeatable Process**
   → Vet deals the same way every time.
   → Process removes emotion and it builds confidence.
4. **Plan for the Downside**
   → What's the worst-case scenario? Can you live with it?
   → If yes, move forward. If not, walk.
5. **Detach from the Outcome**
   → Control the inputs. Let go of the rest.
   → The best investors aren't perfect—they're consistent.

Scarcity Says "Protect." Strategy Says "Grow."

Most of us were raised on scarcity slogans:

- "Money doesn't grow on trees."
- "Be glad you have a steady job."
- "Don't risk what you've got."

That wiring pushes us to:

- Avoid risk instead of understanding it
- Hoard instead of allocate
- React emotionally instead of executing a plan

But strategy is different.

Strategy isn't afraid of risk—it works with it.

▶ The red flag?
When your investing habits are driven by old fears instead of future goals.

Final Thought:

Let the people who are scared stay scared.
You've got a system now.
You've got a framework.
You've got a plan.

You're not playing defense anymore.
You're building.

And when the next storm hits?
You'll be ready—not because you avoided risk...
But because you respected it—and built accordingly.

CHAPTER 14
THE RED FLAGS THAT DERAIL THE LONG GAME

Why Most Investors Fail—and How to Stay in the Game

We've covered the tactics—stocks, real estate, oil, due diligence, tax strategy.
But none of it matters if you can't stay in the game.

Because here's the truth no one likes to hear:
Wealth is built slowly... then suddenly.

It doesn't come from getting lucky.
It comes from avoiding the wrong bets—and staying consistent long enough to let the right ones compound.

▶ Red Flag #1: Chasing Fast Wins

Everyone wants to get rich quick.
But lasting wealth? It's earned through boring consistency:

- Reinvesting cash flow
- Holding quality assets
- Avoiding emotional decisions

The red flag?
Jumping ship too soon.

Every time you sell out of fear, or switch strategies out of boredom, you reset the compounding clock.
Compounding isn't just a financial tool—it's a discipline.

▶ Red Flag #2: Instant Gratification

Delayed gratification is the foundation of real wealth.

The wealthiest people I know:

- Think in decades, not days
- Buy assets, not toys
- Choose ownership, not consumption

They're not immune to temptation. They've just built a system that protects them from themselves.

The red flag?
Buying to impress instead of investing to progress.

▶ Red Flag #3: Overcomplicating the Strategy

The more complex your plan, the easier it is to abandon.

Stick to the timeless truths:

- Own productive assets
- Manage downside
- Stay patient

Your edge isn't complexity—it's consistency.

The red flag?
Thinking more spreadsheets = more success.
It doesn't.

▶ Red Flag #4: Playing Without Boundaries

The long game isn't just about what you invest in—it's about what you say no to.
Set your rules.
Stick to them.

Because when the market wobbles or a hot trend hits your inbox, your emotions will try to take over.
Discipline is your defense.

The red flag?
Investing outside your filters because "this one feels different."
That's how even smart investors get burned.

▶ Red Flag #5: Sitting on the Sideline Too Long

Sometimes, the biggest risk isn't a bad deal—it's never placing a bet at all.
Analysis paralysis. Waiting for perfect certainty.

But the market moves with or without you.

You don't need to be reckless.
You just need to be ready.

If you've done the work—your due diligence, your risk planning, your self-awareness—then don't let fear talk you out of action.

Final Thoughts: Stay in the Game

Wealth isn't a finish line.
It's a process of learning, adapting, and protecting your mindset through every cycle.

If you:

- Build smart habits
- Spot emotional red flags
- Stick to a long-term vision

You'll look up one day and realize—you built a life of freedom.
Not because you got lucky.
But because you didn't get in your own way.

/ PART VII

🔧 LP TOOLKIT = SUPERPOWER SECTION

CHAPTER 15
THE RED FLAG DEAL REVIEW CHECKLIST

How to Spot Risk, Dig Past the Pro Forma, and Avoid the Deals That Burn LPs

Most deals look great on paper.
Glossy pitch decks. Drone-shot videos. Smiling families in sunny courtyards. Clean spreadsheets filled with "conservative" assumptions.

But here's the truth most new LPs don't learn until it's too late: Deals don't go bad because of spreadsheets—they go bad because investors ignore red flags.

This chapter isn't just a checklist.
It's your bullsht *detector*.
It's a tactical playbook for spotting subtle warning signs, decoding the optimism baked into every pitch, and asking the questions most passive investors forget to ask—until it's too late.

You don't need to be an underwriter.
You just need to know where deals usually crack—and how to protect your capital before it's at risk.

🔍 Section 1: Business Plan—Trust the Plan, Not the Pitch

Questions to Ask:

- What's the investment strategy? (value-add, stabilized, development, etc.)
- What's the hold period?
- What's the exit plan?
- Is the plan realistic based on the current market cycle?

Why It Matters:
Every deal lives or dies by its business plan. The best operators know how to communicate the strategy clearly—what they're doing, why they're doing it, and how they're going to make it happen. If it sounds vague, it probably is.

▶ **Red Flag:** Buzzwords like "operational improvements" or "optimization" with no specific action plan or timeline.

Real Example:
One sponsor promised "significant upside" in a 1980s property through "light renovations" and "improved management." But they never specified what the renovations were or how they'd change tenant quality. Two years in, turnover remained high, the renovation budget ballooned, and the sponsor quietly refinanced to avoid a capital call. The plan didn't fail. There was no plan.

Pro Tip:
If a sponsor can't walk you through the first 90 days post-acquisition, that's a problem. That's when the real work starts.

Section 2: Market & Location—Where Good Deals Go to Die

Questions to Ask:

- What's the job and population growth trend?

- What are the local economic drivers?
- What submarket is this really in?
- Are rent comps and vacancy rates realistic?

Why It Matters:
You're not investing in a spreadsheet—you're investing in a real property in a real zip code. A great metro doesn't protect you from a weak submarket. "Booming" markets can turn on a dime if they're over-reliant on one employer or industry.

🔍 **Tip:** Use Google Maps, Apartments.com, and Census data. Pull comps. Look at walkability. Research economic development plans.

Real-World Tactic:
On Apartments.com, set a 2-mile radius around the property and look at current listings for the same number of bedrooms. If your sponsor is projecting $1,800 for a two-bedroom and every other comp is sitting at $1,350—you've got a problem.

Sneaky Red Flag:
Claiming "we're just under market rents" without disclosing why. If a property's rents are already lower than comps, it could be because of deferred maintenance, crime issues, or a tenant base that's hard to stabilize. Don't assume it's an opportunity. Assume it's a reason.

Section 3: Underwriting—The Spreadsheet Is Lying to You

Questions to Ask:

- What are the projected IRR, cash-on-cash, and equity multiple?
- Are rent growth assumptions realistic?
- Is the exit cap rate higher than the entry cap?
- What's the breakeven occupancy?
- Are reserves and contingencies built in?

Why It Matters:
Underwriting is where the optimism gets baked in. Many investors skim the return projections and stop asking questions once they see double-digit IRRs. Don't fall for it.

▶ **Red Flag:** Returns that depend on rent growth or exit cap rates that have no historical precedent.

The Gut-Check Math Test:

1. IRR >17%? → Ask: Is that mostly from a backend sale? If so, what happens if they can't exit on time?
2. Exit Cap = Entry Cap? → Ask: Why? In today's volatile interest rate market, that's a stretch.
3. Rent Growth >5% annually? → Ask: Based on what comps? What's the historical average in that zip code?

LP Mini-Test:
Ask the sponsor for a "stress test" of their model. If they can't show you the deal still works with 10% lower rent growth or a delayed refinance, they're selling you fantasy.

Section 4: Sponsor—You're Not Betting on the Deal. You're Betting on Them.

Questions to Ask:

- How many full-cycle deals have you completed?
- What went wrong in your last project?
- How much of your own money is in this deal?
- Who handles asset management and property management?

Why It Matters:
Track record is helpful. But behavior is everything. You want sponsors who are experienced, humble, and transparent. The best ones volunteer what went wrong—and how they've learned from it.

▶ **Red Flag:** Sponsors who avoid hard questions, dodge past failures, or inflate their role in past wins.

Pro Tip:
Ask to speak to a past investor. Not the one giving the glowing testimonial. A real one, who's been through at least one full cycle with them.

Section 5: Deal Structure—Death by a Thousand Fees

Questions to Ask:

- What's the equity split? (70/30, 80/20, etc.)
- Is there a preferred return?
- What fees are charged?
- Is there a waterfall structure?

Why It Matters:
Some deals look great until you realize the sponsor gets paid no matter what—and you only get paid if everything goes perfectly.

▶ **Red Flag:** Stacked fees and vague promote structures that make it hard to tell who gets what—and when.

Fee Breakdown to Watch:

- **Acquisition Fee:** 1–3% is normal. More? Ask why.
- **Asset Management Fee:** 1–2% of revenue. Is it performance-based?
- **Refi or Exit Fee:** Only acceptable if they create real value.

LP Trick:
Ask for a pro forma showing what happens if the deal underperforms. How much does the GP still make?

Section 6: Reporting—Ghosted After You Wire the Money

Questions to Ask:

- How often will I receive updates?
- What's in each report?
- Is there an investor portal?
- When are K-1s delivered?

Why It Matters:
The #1 complaint LPs have post-investment? Silence. Lack of updates. Late K-1s. You're not just investing your money—you're trusting your sponsor to keep you informed.

▶ **Red Flag:** Sponsors who say "quarterly updates" on a heavy-lift project. You deserve better.

☑ Final Red Flag Scan: 5 Fast Filters

Short on time? Run every deal through these 5 questions:

1. Do I trust the sponsor—especially under pressure?
2. Does the business plan make sense in this market?
3. Are the assumptions grounded—or optimistic?
4. Are the fees fair and transparent?
5. Do I clearly understand how and when I get paid?

If the answer to any of these is fuzzy? Ask again. Or pass.

Digging Deeper: Where Risk Likes to Hide

Even smart investors miss the red flags that don't show up in a deck. Here are five places risk hides out:

1. **Property Management**
   ▶ Value-add deal + W-2 sponsor doing PM themselves? That's not execution—it's ego.
2. **CapEx Budget**
   Who walked the units? Who priced the work? A $6K/unit renovation budget without bids = investor liability.
3. **Rent Roll**
   High delinquency? Rapid turnover? That cash flow you're counting on may already be leaking.
4. **Property Taxes**
   Most counties reassess post-sale. Did the sponsor call the assessor—or just guess?
5. **Who Built the Model**
   Was it a partner or someone fresh out of a bootcamp? The model *is* the deal. Don't treat it like a formality.

5 Killer Questions That Expose Red Flags Instantly

Ask these questions live. Watch the body language. Listen for hesitation.

1. "What went wrong in your last deal—and what did you learn?"
2. "If interest rates rise again, what's your Plan B?"
3. "What assumptions would have to go right for this deal to succeed?"
4. "Can you show me where LPs get paid in a soft exit scenario?"
5. "Who exactly is operating the property—and what's their track record?"

If the answers are tight, clear, and honest—you're dealing with pros. If you get spin, buzzwords, or deflection?
▶ You just found your red flag.

Final Thought

Great decks don't build wealth. Disciplined decisions do.

Your job isn't to say yes to every deal.
It's to say yes to the right ones.

Where:

- The assumptions are real
- The risk is priced in
- The operators have done it before
- And the red flags are minimal—not multiplying

Use this checklist like a radar. You don't have to be perfect. You just have to be alert.

CHAPTER 16
SPOT THE JOCKEY—BEFORE YOU BET THE FARM

How to Vet Sponsors, Uncover Red Flags, and Protect Your Capital

In every syndication, you're betting on two things:
- ♀ The deal (the horse)
- ♀ The operator (the jockey)

But make no mistake—the jockey matters more.

A great operator can salvage a bad deal.
A bad operator can destroy a great one.

That's why the first red flag isn't in the pro forma or the photos. It's in the person pitching you the deal.

This chapter arms you with a tactical framework for sponsor evaluation—what to ask, what to verify, and what to walk away from. Because trust isn't a gut feeling—it's a checklist.

Red Flag Principles for Sponsor Evaluation

Before we get tactical, let's set the foundation:

- Past performance isn't a guarantee—but patterns matter.

One good deal doesn't prove anything. But five tells you something.
- **Transparency isn't a perk—it's a prerequisite.**
If they're hiding small things, what else are they hiding?
- **Hype isn't a strategy—alignment is.**
The best sponsors care about managing downside, not maximizing optics.
- **Charisma can't manage your investment. Operational discipline can.**
Smooth talk won't fix bad plumbing or lazy management.

🔍 Check the Receipts: How to Uncover Red Flags

If you're wiring money into a deal, do the work.
Don't just take their word for it—verify everything.

☑ SEC Enforcement Database
sec.gov/litigation/litreleases.htm
Use Ctrl+F or the site's search bar. Look for prior civil actions.

☑ SEC EDGAR Filings
sec.gov/edgar/search
Search by full name. Focus on 506(b), 506(c), or Reg A offerings and administrative actions.

☑ Google Site Search Hack
Search: site:sec.gov "[Full Name]" enforcement action
Sometimes faster and more complete than EDGAR.

☑ PACER (Federal Court Records)
pacer.uscourts.gov
Search for lawsuits tied to fraud, misrepresentation, bankruptcy, or investor disputes.

☑ FINRA BrokerCheck
brokercheck.finra.org

Only applies to registered reps—but still worth checking.

☑ State Securities Regulators

Google your state's securities commission to check for fines, suspensions, or cease-and-desist orders.

▶ **Red Flag:** If a sponsor resists this level of scrutiny or gets defensive—walk away.
Legit operators expect due diligence. Great ones welcome it.

▶ The Sponsor Red Flag Worksheet

Here's your interview framework. Ask these questions—and pay close attention not just to what they say, but how they say it.

Category	Ask These Questions	What to Watch For
Track Record	- How many full-cycle deals? - Actual vs. projected returns? - What asset class?	Specifics, not spin. Patterns over performance.
Experience	- How long in real estate? - What was your background before syndications? - Managed through a downturn?	Battle scars, not just bull markets.
Skin in the Game	- How much capital of your own is in the deal? - Are you signing the loan?	No skin = no alignment. Beware, low exposure.
Communication	- How often do you update LPs? - Can I see a sample report? - Do you use a portal?	Proactive, consistent, organized.
Operations	- Who manages the asset day-to-day? - What KPIs do you track weekly? - How do you respond to surprises?	Process matters. Execution wins deals.

THE RED FLAG PLAYBOOK

Category	Ask These Questions	What to Watch For
Transparency	- What's your worst deal—and what did you learn? - Any pending lawsuits? - Can I talk to a past LP?	You want honesty and accountability.
Fees & Structure	- What fees do you charge? - Is there a preferred return? - How does profit split work?	Clean, simple terms. No gotchas.
Exit Plan	- What's the planned hold period? - Is a 1031 or refi on the table? - What's your contingency if cap rates spike?	Adaptability over rigidity.

Real Red Flags (And Why They Matter)

Red Flag	Why It Matters
Vague or evasive answers	Evasion hides risk. Clarity builds trust.
No skin in the game	If they win either way, you might lose.
Great branding, no track record	Don't fund the Instagram dream.
Inconsistent LP updates	Poor ops = investor frustration and mistrust.
Fee-heavy structures	Misaligned incentives = red alert.
Won't share performance history	If it's good, they'll tell you. If not—they'll dodge.

💡 Case Study: The Charismatic Sponsor with a Silent Collapse

An LP invested $100,000 in a Texas-based multifamily deal. The sponsor had a polished deck, strong social presence, and a "proven model." But there was no breakdown of how previous deals performed—and no third-party property manager listed.

The red flag?
All communication went through the sponsor's spouse. Updates were irregular. Expenses ballooned. And in year two, the sponsor

quietly refinanced, pulled out equity, and paid themselves—but cut LP distributions by 50%.

Lesson: Charisma is cheap. Clarity and structure matter more.

What Drives the GP Drives Your Outcome

Every sponsor optimizes for something. If you can't figure out what that is—you're the one being optimized.

If the GP Optimizes For...	You Can Expect...
IRR	Faster exits, shorter holds, potential volatility
Equity Multiple	Longer holds, less focus on annualized returns
Cash-on-Cash	Higher distributions now, lower backend potential
After-Tax Returns	Heavy use of cost seg and depreciation strategies

▶ **Red Flag Matchup:**
If you want steady cash flow but the GP reinvests every dollar—they're not wrong, but you're misaligned.
If you want a long-term hold and they exit in three years? That's a problem waiting to happen.

Ask. Confirm. Document.

Bonus Questions to Reveal Red Flags

Ask these live—or over email—and read between the lines:

- "What's your biggest lesson from a failed deal?"
- "How do you communicate when returns miss projections?"
- "Who do I contact if I have questions after closing?"
- "What would make you walk away from a deal during due diligence?"
- "How do you define success in your LP relationships?"

Their answers will tell you more than the pitch ever will.

Behavior Patterns: Great vs. Problem Sponsors

Scenario	Great Sponsors Do This	Red Flag Sponsors Do This
Deal goes sideways	Communicate early, revise plan, protect LPs	Delay updates, blame others, dodge questions
Returns miss target	Own it, explain it, adjust next deal	Ghost LPs, reframe it as a "market issue"
Asked tough questions	Welcome them, provide specifics	Get defensive or pivot the conversation
K-1s delayed	Explain cause, give delivery timeline	Say nothing until you complain
Asked for past LP reference	Offer 2–3 without hesitation	"I'll get back to you" = won't

Final Thought: Bet on the Jockey—But Only After a Full Vet

You wouldn't fund a startup without grilling the founder.
You shouldn't fund a syndication without grilling the sponsor.

- Ask the hard questions.
- Don't confuse confidence with competence.
- Trust your gut—but only after you've checked their track record, references, and red flag responses.

Markets shift. Deals fall apart. But great operators?
They adapt.
They communicate.
They protect capital—even if it costs them personally.

▶ This chapter isn't about paranoia.
It's about **pattern recognition**.

Because when things go wrong, the red flags were almost always there.
You just have to know how to spot them.

CHAPTER 17
ASK LIKE YOUR WEALTH DEPENDS ON IT

Smart Questions That Uncover Red Flags Before You Wire the Money

An LP call isn't just a formality.
It's your moment to peel back the pitch and evaluate the people behind the promise.

Most sponsors expect softball questions:
"What's the target IRR?"
"How long is the hold?"
"How soon do we start distributions?"

But smart LPs don't stop there.
They ask sharper questions—strategic ones.
The kind that flush out red flags before the deal goes sideways.
You're not just gathering facts—you're evaluating character, competence, and crisis behavior.

This chapter gives you a battle-tested list of questions to use on every LP call—plus the red flags to listen for between the lines.

Section 1: Sponsor Track Record & Real-World Experience

Goal: Spot patterns of success—or patterns in how they handle failure.

Ask:

- "How many full-cycle deals have you completed?"
- "What were the projected vs. actual returns on your last three exits?"
- "Tell me about a deal that underperformed—what went wrong, and what did you learn?"
- "How has your underwriting changed in the last three years?"

Listen For:

- Real numbers, not vague marketing language
- Willingness to discuss losses—without spinning them
- Evolution in thinking and process as markets shifted

▶ **Red Flag:** "We haven't had any deals underperform."
(That's either untrue—or they haven't done enough deals.)

Pro Move: Ask to see a sample closing summary or investor update from a bad deal. Their tone will tell you everything about how they lead when things go sideways.

Section 2: Risk Management Strategy

Goal: See if they plan for downside—or just assume things go right.

Ask:

- "What are the biggest risks in this deal—and how are you mitigating them?"
- "What's your breakeven occupancy?"

- "How are you protecting against interest rate or cap rate risk?"
- "What reserves are built in—and how long would they last in a downturn?"

Listen For:

- Specific contingency plans—not vague confidence
- Deep knowledge of debt terms, rate caps, and liquidity buffers
- Humility about what they don't control

▶ **Red Flag:** "We're confident in the upside."
Confidence isn't a strategy. Reserves are.

Case Study:
One sponsor in 2022 said they weren't worried about rate caps because "we're getting a deal on the front end." By 2023, their variable-rate debt ballooned, and they halted distributions. They hadn't bought a rate cap. They hadn't modeled interest rate shocks. LPs who asked about rate strategy walked. Those who didn't? Paid for it.

Section 3: Operations & Execution

Goal: Understand who's running the playbook after closing.

Ask:

- "Who's managing the property day to day?"
- "Is property management in-house or third-party?"
- "What KPIs do you track weekly or monthly?"
- "What happens if projections start to slip?"

Listen For:

- Specific names and accountability—not "we outsource that"

- Clarity around renovations, lease-up, occupancy targets, expense control
- Emphasis on execution, not just acquisition

▶ **Red Flag:** They can buy deals—but can't run them.
Follow-Up Question: "How do you track renovation progress? Can I see a sample dashboard?"
You don't need to audit it. You just want to know it exists.

Section 4: Communication & Investor Relations

Goal: Set the tone early—how they treat you when things are going well and when they're not.

Ask:

- "How often will I receive updates—and what will they include?"
- "When do you send K-1s?"
- "Do you use an investor portal?"
- "Can I see a sample update or prior report?"

Listen For:

- Consistency and professionalism
- Use of tech tools to streamline reporting
- Transparency about previous misses or communication lapses

▶ **Red Flag:** "We usually update quarterly, but during renovations we'll send things as needed."
Translation: You'll be chasing them for information.

Pro Move: Ask, "What's the last thing an LP pushed back on—and how did you handle it?"

Section 5: Alignment, Incentives & Deal Structure

Goal: Know how they get paid—and when you do.

Ask:

- "How much personal capital are you investing in this deal?"
- "Can you walk me through the fee structure and waterfall?"
- "When do you start participating in profits?"
- "If the deal underperforms, who gets paid first?"

Listen For:

- Real skin in the game (cash, not just effort)
- Transparent fees—no junk line items or buried splits
- Clarity around preferred return mechanics
- Willingness to forgo pay if the deal struggles

▶ **Red Flag:** They win no matter what. You only win if they hit a home run.

Section 6: What Great Answers Actually Sound Like

Let's look at sample answers—and what they reveal.

Question: "What's your biggest lesson from a failed deal?"
- ☑ Strong: "In 2021, we bought a C-class asset in a gentrifying area. Our rent comps were too aggressive, and we missed by 15%. We've since changed our underwriting to only use in-place rents unless physical upgrades are clearly documented."
- ▶ Weak: "We haven't really had any issues—maybe a little delay here or there."

THE RED FLAG PLAYBOOK

Question: "Can you explain your fee structure?"
- ☑ Strong: "2% acquisition, 2% asset management, 70/30 split after a 7% preferred return. No disposition fee."
- ▶ Weak: "We're pretty standard, just a few fees here and there—it's all in the deck."

Question: "What KPIs do you track weekly?"
- ☑ Strong: "Occupancy, lease trade-out, delinquency, CapEx schedule, and NOI variance."
- ▶ Weak: "We keep an eye on occupancy and expenses."

The Post-Call Debrief: What to Write Down After Every Call

After each LP call, jot these down:

1. Three things that impressed you.
2. Two things that didn't sit right—but weren't dealbreakers.
3. One big unknown or fuzzy answer.
4. Gut check: Would I trust this person in a crisis?

Patterns will emerge. And when you compare across sponsors, your BS radar gets sharper.

🔍 The LP Question Stack (How to Go Deeper, Fast)

Want to dig deeper without sounding aggressive? Stack your questions:

1. Start soft: "What's your rent growth assumption?"
2. Follow-up: "What comps did you use to support that?"
3. Then push: "How does that compare to trailing 12-months in that zip code?"

A good sponsor answers all three without flinching.
A shaky one stumbles on the second and evades the third.

▶ Bonus Red Flag Questions (When You Want to Go Deep)

Ask these when the call is going well—or when you're unsure about the sponsor's maturity:

- "What would make you walk away from a deal—even after LOI?"
- "What triggers an exit decision—and who decides?"
- "What's your long-term plan: building a fund, a firm, or a legacy?"
- "If this deal underdelivers, what does that mean for your brand?"

▶ **Red Flag:** If they fumble these questions or get defensive—that's your answer.

Pro Insight: The best sponsors have wrestled with these ideas. Their answers might not be perfect—but they'll be real.

🎯 Final Thought: This Isn't Just a Deal—It's a Relationship

Most LPs ask like they're trying to qualify a deal.
But the smartest ones ask like they're hiring a co-pilot.
Because they are.

A syndication is a relationship—not a product.
You're not evaluating a property.
You're evaluating the decision-maker who controls everything after you wire the money.

Great sponsors welcome tough questions.
They expect scrutiny.
They respect discipline.
They don't deflect.
They don't dance.
They answer—clearly.

Because they know something most investors forget:
Your capital isn't just fuel.

It's a vote of confidence.
And real operators treat that vote like it matters.

So don't apologize for asking hard questions.
Ask like your wealth depends on it—because it does.

CHAPTER 18
HOW AI IS RESHAPING REAL ESTATE—AND REVEALING RED FLAGS IN PLAIN SIGHT

From Gut Instinct to Ground Truth with Placer.ai, Satellite Data, and Behavioral Analytics

Real estate used to be a boots-on-the-ground game.
You drove the property. You talked to the tenants. You counted cars in the parking lot.
You guessed, inferred, assumed.

Today, you can know.

Thanks to AI-powered platforms like Placer.ai, Orbital Insight, Regrid, Zoning.ai, Near Intelligence, PiinPoint, and UrbanFootprint, passive investors can now tap into real-time foot traffic, zoning shifts, behavioral segmentation, and tenant movement—without ever stepping foot on-site.

These tools are changing the game for GPs.
But for LPs?
They're a red flag detection system hiding in plain sight.

Who's Who in the AI Real Estate Stack

Let's expand the toolkit:

Placer.ai
Foot traffic trends, dwell times, anchor performance, and visitor frequency by property.

Orbital Insight
Satellite image analysis for parking lot volume, vehicle counts, roof aging, development activity, and night-light tracking (a proxy for economic vibrancy).

Zoning.ai
AI-powered zoning compliance and land-use mapping. Critical for development or repositioning projects.

Regrid / LandGlide
Parcel data, land ownership, tax maps, and zoning overlays—accessible in seconds.

Near Intelligence (formerly UberMedia)
Tracks movement patterns, competitive visitation, cross-shopping, and retail cannibalization risks.

Spatial.ai
Psychographic segmentation using social behavior and geotagged digital content. Reveals how people think and spend—not just where they live.

Claritas
Deep demographic and spending behavior modeling. Helps LPs test sponsor assumptions about tenant base and pricing strategy.

PiinPoint
Retail site selection analytics using AI to forecast customer demand, trade areas, and co-tenancy success.

UrbanFootprint
Macro view of urban movement, climate exposure, and demographic trends. Useful for stress-testing long-term assumptions.

▶ Red Flags You Can Spot with AI Tools

Red Flag #1: "Great Location" with No Data to Back It Up
Use Placer.ai or Near Intelligence to measure real traffic and trendlines.
If foot traffic is falling—or the anchor tenant is losing visits year over year—there's a disconnect between pitch and reality.

Red Flag #2: Psychographic Mismatch
Platforms like Spatial.ai or Claritas show whether the population's income, behavior, and preferences align with the sponsor's plan. Mismatch = red flag.

Red Flag #3: Phantom Tenants or Problematic Anchors
Use PiinPoint or Placer.ai to track tenant health and synergy.
Is the grocery anchor still pulling consistent volume? Is the adjacent strip mall siphoning traffic?

Red Flag #4: Land-Use or Zoning Surprises
Regrid and Zoning.ai can alert you to parcels that have usage restrictions, require variances, or are zoned in conflict with the stated business plan.
For development deals, this is mission-critical.

Red Flag #5: No Post-Acquisition Monitoring
If the sponsor stops using AI after they close, they're flying blind.
Ask: *What post-close indicators do you track to know if the business plan is working?*

Red Flag #6: Assumptions with No "What-If" Scenario Testing

Use ChatGPT or AI models to run counter-scenarios.
Ask: *What if rent growth is half what's projected? What if exit cap rates widen?*
If the model breaks quickly—it wasn't strong to begin with.

🔧 Your LP AI Toolkit: From Hype to Application

Tool	Use Case	Red Flag Trigger
Placer.ai	Foot traffic, dwell time, tenant validation	Declining visits, anchor erosion
Orbital Insight	Satellite view of parking lots, night light data	Empty lots, aging roofs, stalled construction
Zoning.ai	Confirm zoning, land use permissions	Repositioning risk, entitlement mismatch
Regrid	Parcel ownership and compliance	Ownership issues, overlapping parcels
Claritas	Demographic-spending analysis	Income doesn't support proposed rents
Spatial.ai	Psychographics, lifestyle segmentation	Tenant mix doesn't match behavior
PiinPoint	Retail health and trade area validation	Underperforming co-tenants, low pull radius
UrbanFootprint	Long-term macro trends and climate overlays	Flood/fire exposure, poor future migration trends

AI-Enhanced Sponsor Questions

Ask this:
☑ "What AI tools do you use to validate foot traffic, demographic fit, and competitive risk?"
Not that:
✗ "Do you think it's a good retail corridor?"

Ask this:
☑ "How do you monitor asset performance in real time post-close?"

Not that:
✘ "Will you send us quarterly reports?"

Ask this:
☑ "Can you share Placer or Orbital data for this location?"
Not that:
✘ "Have you seen this center lately?"

Final Thought: Use AI to Confirm—or Confront—the Narrative

No tech will ever replace sound judgment.
But the best LPs use these tools to interrogate, not just observe.

Because while a pitch deck tells you what the sponsor *wants* you to see...
AI tells you what's *actually* happening on the ground.

That's the difference between a gut feeling and a data-backed decision.
And in today's environment, smart LPs know:
Red flags aren't buried. They're just waiting to be uncovered.

CHAPTER 19
WHERE TO START

A Tactical Roadmap for New and Emerging LPs

By now, you've seen how powerful passive investing can be—and how many hidden risks (and rewards) live beneath the surface.

But here's the question almost everyone asks after reading a book like this:
"What do I do next?"

The answer depends on where you are in your journey. So let's ditch the one-size-fits-all approach and build a roadmap that meets you exactly where you are.

Whether you're new, curious, or ready to commit capital—this chapter will help you move forward with clarity, confidence, and caution.

Stage 1: The Learning LP

(You're building your foundation. No rush.)

You might still be asking:
- What's a K-1?
- What exactly does a GP do?
- What's the risk if this goes south?

This is a good place to be. It means you're thinking before jumping.

Tactical Steps:
- Start building your education library.
  Revisit Chapters 6 through 9. These are your red flag radar.

- Understand accreditation.
  Are you an accredited investor under SEC rules? If not, start by understanding Reg A and 506(b) offerings.

- Subscribe to 3–5 sponsor email lists.
  Watch how they communicate, how often they send deals, and what kind of language they use. Don't invest yet—just observe.

- Create your "Deal Journal."
  Keep a file (or spreadsheet) where you track deals that catch your eye. What were the projected returns? Did the messaging feel overly aggressive? Were you confused by the terms? Track your reactions—you'll spot patterns fast.

- Talk to a few experienced LPs.
  Ask how they got started, what they wish they'd done differently, and what red flags they missed.

Stage 2: The Evaluating LP

(You're accredited, educated—and cautious.)

This is where many smart investors stall. Not from fear—but from a desire to "get it perfect."
Perfection isn't the goal. **Pattern recognition is.**

Tactical Steps:
- Narrow your focus.
  Choose 1–2 asset classes to study deeply (e.g., multifamily and RV parks). Too much variety early on leads to decision fatigue.

- Pick your 3 key investing filters.
  Examples: Must have preferred return, must be third-party managed, must be cash-flowing day one. These are your dealbreakers. Stick to them.

- Use the Sponsor Evaluation Worksheet (Chapter 16).
  Don't just look at deals—start with the person behind them. Look up their name in the SEC database. Ask for references. Read between the lines.

- Review deals without investing (yet).
  Download 5–10 pitch decks and underwrite them lightly. Compare rent growth assumptions, exit cap rate logic, and debt structure. Ask sponsors for clarification—even if you're not investing yet. See how they respond.

- Ask better questions.
  Use Chapter 17. Print it. Ask the uncomfortable questions. Not every LP does—and that's why not every LP wins.

Stage 3: The Committed LP

(You're ready to wire money—but doing it with intention.)

This is the moment where education turns into action. And it's where most red flags show up.

Tactical Steps:
- Review your investment thesis.
  Ask: "Does this deal match my strategy—or am I chasing returns?"

- Ask for the full legal packet.
  Don't invest off the pitch deck. Read the PPM. Review the operating agreement. Understand your rights as an LP.

- Ask for a past investor to talk to.
Especially one who's gone full cycle—you'll learn more from that 10-minute call than from any pitch deck.

- Create a capital allocation plan.
Example: $250K available. $50K per deal. 5 operators. 3 asset classes. This forces diversification and reduces emotional decision-making.

- Know your "no-go" red flags.
Write them down. For example: No preferred return? Walk. IRR >20% with no detail on how? Walk. All returns from backend refi or sale? Walk.

Real-Life LP Pathways

Ashley, the Tech Exec (The Evaluating LP)
Ashley was an accredited investor from tech IPO equity. She spent 18 months learning—subscribed to five sponsor lists, joined a real estate forum, and built a deal journal. When she finally wired her first $50K, she had reviewed 12 deals, interviewed three past LPs, and written her own LP playbook.

"I wasn't scared—I was selective. That's a big difference."

Carlos, the Business Owner (The Burned-Then-Better LP)
Carlos jumped into his first syndication with a flashy sponsor and a 21% projected IRR. He didn't ask about debt structure or cash reserves. When interest rates spiked, the sponsor paused distributions and refinanced into worse terms—just to pay themselves.
Now Carlos uses a 7-point vetting system and shares it with friends.

"I don't mind a deal underperforming. But don't tell me it's 'still on track' when it's clearly not."

Michelle, the Dentist (The Collaborative LP)
Michelle created a small "LP circle" of three friends. Each reviews the same deal separately, then they meet to compare notes. One friend usually catches something the others miss. She credits the circle for helping her avoid two high-risk deals that had red flags in the fee structure.

"It's not about paranoia—it's about pattern recognition."

✗ 5 LP Mistakes to Avoid (Now Expanded with Examples)

1. Chasing IRR Over Operator Quality
It's easy to get lured by a 20% IRR—but who's delivering it?
▦ *Real Example:* One sponsor projected 19.6% IRR with a 3-year flip. But their last three deals missed projections and paid out late. LPs were still swayed by the number—only to realize it was built on a refinance that never happened.
☑ *Correction:* Look at past actuals. If a sponsor doesn't volunteer them, that's your cue.

2. Not Asking for Past Investor References
You'd never hire a contractor without reviews. Why do it with your capital?
☎ *Tactical Move:* Ask, "Can I talk to someone who's gone full cycle with you—one who made money and one who didn't?" The answers will be gold.
☑ *Correction:* If the sponsor fumbles this question, you just found your answer.

3. Going All In On a Single Deal
First-time LPs often pick one sponsor, one deal, and put 100% of their capital behind it.
⚠ *Real Risk:* If that sponsor goes dark, so does your money. If that market softens, your timeline gets pushed.
☑ *Correction:* 3 sponsors. 3 markets. 3 different deal types. That's how pros spread exposure.

4. Ignoring the Tax Trap at Exit

Many LPs enjoy "paper losses" through depreciation—but forget about recapture at exit.

📋 *Real Case:* One LP received $20K in distributions over 3 years—then got hit with a $12K tax bill upon sale. Why? Depreciation recapture and no losses elsewhere to offset it.

☑ *Correction:* Talk to your CPA before you invest. Not after.

5. Assuming Distributions Will Be Fixed or Immediate

Distributions depend on occupancy, renovation schedules, leasing velocity, and loan terms.

🔄 *Real Talk:* A property may be 95% occupied but still cash-flow negative during renovations or repositioning. Preferred returns accrue—but may not be paid monthly.

☑ *Correction:* Ask: "What's your distribution schedule—and what would delay it?" Get the real answer upfront.

💭 How to Build Your LP Investment Thesis

Want to level up fast? Write your personal LP investment thesis—a one-page summary of how you'll make decisions going forward.

Include:

- **Capital Allocation Plan**
  (How much, per deal, across how many operators)
- **Asset Class Preference**
  (Multifamily? Energy? Self-storage? Why?)
- **Risk Profile**
  (Are you chasing growth, cash flow, or tax savings?)
- **Deal Structure Preferences**
  (Preferred return? Equity splits? Hold periods?)
- **Hard Red Flags**
  (No third-party PM, no skin in the game, no full-cycle history = no go)

Print it. Keep it next to your laptop. Reference it every time a new deal hits your inbox.

🧠 Final Thought

Being a limited partner doesn't mean being a passive thinker.
It means being intentional—with your questions, your capital, and your partners.

You're not picking stocks.
You're choosing strategies, structures, and people.

Mistakes will happen. That's okay. But when you go in with clarity, ask smarter questions, and learn from the red flags of others—you'll move faster, with more confidence and less regret.

That's how real wealth is built—**one informed decision at a time.**

✉ Need Help?

Still have questions? Want a second set of eyes on a deal?
Reach out anytime: **carson@passive.investments**
You don't have to figure this out alone.

PART VI
BONUS TAX TRAPS AND STRATEGIC ADVANTAGES

CHAPTER 20
TAX STRATEGY FOR LPS—DEPRECIATION, K-1S, AND RED FLAGS

Let's be honest—nobody enjoys paying taxes.

But here's a red flag most investors miss: They overpay year after year simply because they don't understand how to legally reduce their burden.

The U.S. tax code isn't just a rulebook. It's a roadmap—one that rewards people who build, own, and invest in the infrastructure this country needs. And real estate syndications, when done right, let you tap into the same strategies used by professional landlords and full-time developers.

In this chapter, you'll learn how depreciation, paper losses, and K-1s can help you grow your wealth by keeping more of what you earn—and how to avoid the red flags that can sabotage those benefits.

Why Real Estate Is So Tax-Friendly

Real estate holds a privileged place in the tax code because it provides essential infrastructure. The government wants more housing. More warehouses. More energy infrastructure. So it creates incentives for those willing to invest in them—especially private capital.

These incentives come in the form of:

- **Depreciation**
- **Cost segregation**
- **Bonus depreciation**
- **1031 exchanges**
- **Opportunity Zones**
- **Favorable long-term capital gains treatment**

Put simply: You can often **earn income today while deferring taxes for years.**

🏛 *Government-Backed Wealth Creation*

This isn't a loophole—it's intentional. When you fund a deal that creates housing, logistics capacity, or energy reliability, the IRS effectively says:

"Thanks for helping. Keep more of your money."

And this is the first mindset shift most LPs need to make:
Tax savings aren't an afterthought. They're a core part of your total return.

The Power of Paper Losses

This is what makes real estate investing so different from traditional stock or bond investing:

You can make money and report a loss.

Let's break that down.

🧾 *Example: Real Cash, Paper Loss*

You invest $100,000 into a value-add apartment syndication. In Year 1:

- You receive $7,000 in distributions.
- Your K-1 shows a **($30,000)** passive loss.

That's not a mistake. That's the power of **accelerated depreciation**.

Even though you're making money, the depreciation expense creates a **"paper loss"** that shelters that income.

If you have other passive income—rental properties, royalties, other syndications—it might offset those as well.

🔍 *What Can Be Offset with Paper Losses?*

- Net cash flow from rentals
- Other K-1 distributions
- Royalty income from books, music, or patents
- Gains from passive business interests (LLCs, funds)

▶ **Red Flag: Misreading Your K-1**

First-time LPs often panic when they see a large negative number.

They assume:

"Wait—this deal is losing money!"

But that negative number is **exactly what you want** in many cases.

If your CPA doesn't explain that—or worse, flags it as a problem—you're working with the wrong professional.

☑ **Always work with a real estate-focused CPA.** If they don't know how to interpret a K-1, you could lose out on thousands in legal deductions.

Active vs. Passive Income: Know the Categories

Real estate syndications are **passive investments by default**. That's good for tax efficiency—but it limits how those losses can be applied.

🔄 *Exception 1: Real Estate Professional Status (REP)*

If you or your spouse qualifies as a **Real Estate Professional**, you can use those paper losses to offset **active** income like W-2 wages or business income.

To qualify, you must:

- Spend **750+ hours/year** in real estate activities
- **Materially participate** in those activities
- Not have a second full-time job (in most cases)

It's powerful—but not easy to claim. And it's highly audited.

🔄 *Exception 2: Short-Term Rental (STR) Loophole*

STRs (like Airbnb/VRBO) fall into a weird middle ground. In some cases, if you **materially participate** in an STR business, the IRS may let you offset active income without REP status.

But this is nuanced, and the rules are changing rapidly.

▶ Red Flag: Faking REP or STR Status

These are goldmines if used right—but **landmines** if used wrong.

- Simply owning an STR or rental does **not** make you eligible.
- "Material participation" must be documented with logs, schedules, and proof.

If you're claiming REP or STR exemptions, keep meticulous records—and make sure your CPA has handled these before.

Depreciation & Cost Segregation

Depreciation is the foundation of the tax advantage in real estate.

The IRS lets you "wear down" your building over time and write off that loss—even if the building is appreciating in value.

Straight-Line Depreciation

Property Type	Depreciation Period
Residential	27.5 years
Commercial	39 years

This alone creates steady paper losses—but most syndications go further.

What Is Cost Segregation?

A **cost segregation study** breaks down the building into individual components like:

- Appliances, cabinets (5–7 years)
- Pavement, sidewalks, fencing (15 years)
- HVAC, roofs, electrical systems (varies)

This lets you front-load your depreciation and take huge losses in the early years.

Real-World Cost Seg Example

Let's say you invest $100,000.

- The deal includes a cost seg study.

- $40,000 of that investment is allocated to components with accelerated depreciation.
- In Year 1, you get a **$40,000 paper loss**—on a $100K investment.

If you had other passive income, you might wipe out your entire tax bill.

Bonus Depreciation: The Turbo Button

Cost segregation is powerful on its own—but bonus depreciation kicks it into overdrive.

Bonus Depreciation Phase-Out Timeline

Year	Bonus Depreciation
2024	60%
2025	40%
2026	20%
2027	0% (unless extended)

As of mid-2025, Congress is debating whether to reinstate 100% bonus depreciation. But there's no guarantee.

▶ Red Flag: Betting on Congress

If your deal depends on **bonus depreciation being restored**, that's a speculative tax play.

Ask the sponsor:

"What does your tax forecast look like **if bonus depreciation drops to zero?**"

If they don't have a backup plan—you probably need one.

What Is a K-1—And How to Read It

Your **K-1 (Form 1065)** is the tax form you'll receive from each syndication you invest in. It shows:

- Your share of ordinary income or loss
- Depreciation passed through
- Capital account balance
- Distributions you received

Sample K-1 Walkthrough

Let's decode a simple example.

Line Item	Amount	Meaning
Ordinary Income	($25,000)	Paper loss from depreciation
Cash Distributions	$7,000	Real cash paid to you during the year
Capital Contributions	$100,000	Your original investment
Ending Capital Acct	$81,000	Book value after depreciation

Even though you took home $7K in cash, you show a $25K loss. That loss may offset other passive income—or carry forward until a future sale.

Red Flag: Your CPA Doesn't Know How to Read a K-1

If your accountant shrugs, says "I'll just plug this in," and moves on—you could be overpaying by thousands.

☑ **Ask your CPA these 5 questions:**

1. Do you work with other real estate investors?
2. How do you handle depreciation recapture?
3. Can you help me track carryforward losses?
4. Do you advise on REP or STR strategy?

5. What are the red flags I should watch for in this deal?

If they fumble the answers, it's time to upgrade.

What Happens When the Property Sells?

This is where things get tricky—and expensive if you're not careful.

When the asset sells, two things happen:

1. You owe **capital gains tax** on the profit
2. You owe **depreciation recapture** on the paper losses you previously took

Depreciation Recapture 101

- Recapture is taxed up to **25%**
- It applies even if you used passive losses to offset other income
- It can catch LPs off guard who thought the losses were "free"

Ways to Manage the Tax Hit

- **1031 Exchange** (rare for LPs, but possible via TIC)
- **Opportunity Zone reinvestment**
- **Charitable contributions**
- **Offset with capital losses from the stock market**
- **Cash-out refi** instead of sale (no tax on debt)

▶ Red Flag: No Exit Tax Strategy

Ask your sponsor before investing:

"How do you plan to help LPs mitigate capital gains and recapture?"

If their answer is vague—or they say "that's on your CPA"—that's a problem.

FAQs: Tax Strategy for LPs

Q: Do passive losses expire?
A: No. They roll forward indefinitely until you use them.

Q: Can I use these losses to offset my W-2?
A: Only if you (or your spouse) qualify as a Real Estate Professional or STR participant.

Q: Will I owe taxes on distributions if the K-1 shows a loss?
A: Usually not. Distributions are a return of capital until you hit zero basis.

Q: What if I sell my LP interest early?
A: You may owe capital gains based on your adjusted basis. Always consult your CPA before selling.

Quick Reference: K-1 Tax Strategy Cheat Sheet

Concept	What It Means
Depreciation	Non-cash expense reducing taxable income
Cost Segregation	Accelerated write-off of specific components
Bonus Depreciation	One-year write-off (phasing out through 2027)
K-1	Tax form showing income, loss, distributions
Passive Loss Limits	Apply to passive income only (unless REP/STR)
Recapture	Tax owed when you "pay back" depreciation at sale

Final Thoughts: Know the Tools, Avoid the Traps

Syndications don't just grow wealth through appreciation—they **preserve wealth through tax strategy**.

But these tools only work if you:

- Understand your K-1

- Track your passive losses
- Ask the right questions before investing
- Work with tax pros who understand real estate

📌 Why Real Estate Is So Tax-Friendly

💡 Example: Comparing Real Estate to Stocks

Imagine you invest $100K into stocks and earn $7K in dividends. You'll pay taxes on every dollar. No paper losses. No sheltering.

Now, invest $100K into real estate syndications and receive $7K in cash flow... while showing a ($30K) paper loss. One gives you a tax bill. The other gives you a refund or offsets future passive income.

That's why real estate isn't just about returns—it's about efficiency.

💬 Sponsor Question to Ask:

"Do you model after-tax returns for LPs? Can I see the projected passive loss schedule?"

📌 The Power of Paper Losses

💡 How Paper Losses Flow Through

Those passive losses reduce your taxable income **on Schedule E** of your 1040. They don't just disappear—they wait on your tax return and can offset gains for years.

💡 Real Example

A physician invests $100K into three deals and receives:

- $8K in total distributions
- ($85K) in total paper losses
  Her CPA offsets $8K in passive gains from other real estate and rolls the remaining $77K into future tax years. In year

three, a deal sells, and she shields nearly all of her $60K profit with losses she banked earlier.

📊 Passive Loss Carryforward Tracker (Example)

Year	Passive Loss Created	Passive Income Offset	Unused Losses	Cumulative Balance
2023	($30,000)	$5,000	($25,000)	($25,000)
2024	($20,000)	$3,000	($17,000)	($42,000)

📌 Active vs. Passive Income

💡 **Tip:** If you're married and only one spouse has a full-time job, the other might qualify for REP. That opens the door to offsetting **W-2 income** with syndication losses—legally.

🧠 What the IRS Looks For in REP Audits

- Detailed time logs showing >750 hours
- Evidence of material participation (not just ownership)
- No conflicting full-time employment

▶ **Mini Red Flag:** A sponsor or guru tells you "Just check the box" for REP status. That's a fast way to end up audited—and paying back taxes with penalties.

💡 **Ask Your Sponsor:**

"Has a third-party engineering firm been hired to run the cost segregation study?"

If not, depreciation may be underutilized—or non-existent.

▶ **Mini Red Flag:** The sponsor brags about depreciation but can't tell you **how or when** it will be generated.

Bonus Depreciation & Legislation Watch

Legislative Notes:
The push to restore 100% bonus depreciation has bipartisan support but was stuck in gridlock before finally passing the House. Always assume worst-case and evaluate the deal's core fundamentals without it—until it's officially law.

Visual Example: Impact of Bonus Depreciation Phase-Out

Year	Bonus Rate	Paper Loss from $100K Investment
2023	80%	$40,000
2025	40%	$20,000
2027	0%	$6,000 (basic straight-line only)

K-1 Strategy for LPs

Checklist: What to Look for on Your K-1

- Box 1: Ordinary Income (or loss)
- Box 19: Distributions
- Beginning/Ending Capital Account: Basis tracking
- Any state-specific forms (CA, NY, etc.)

▶ **Mini Red Flag:** A K-1 with no Box 1 loss and no depreciation breakdown in a value-add deal—ask why. You may not be getting the full benefits.

What Happens When the Property Sells?

Understanding Recapture Timing
Depreciation recapture happens **whether or not you used the paper losses**. If you got $30K in passive losses and didn't use them, you still owe the tax if the property sells and you profited.

📋 Mini Checklist: Questions to Ask Your CPA Before a Sale

1. What's my estimated capital gain and recapture tax?
2. Can I offset with any capital losses this year?
3. Am I eligible for an Opportunity Zone rollover or charitable strategy?
4. What's my current passive loss carryforward?

🔖 Additional LP FAQs

Q: I received a K-1 after I filed. What now?
A: You may need to file an amended return. Going forward, consider filing extensions until all K-1s are in hand.

Q: What's the best entity to invest through—personal name or LLC?
A: Many LPs invest through LLCs for liability and recordkeeping. But talk to your CPA. Your tax result may not change unless the LLC is treated as a partnership.

Q: Can I use depreciation losses from Deal A to offset gains from Deal B?
A: Yes—if both are passive. That's a major tax advantage of scaling across deals.

▶ Red Flag Analysis Summary Table

Red Flag	Why It Matters	What to Ask
K-1 losses misunderstood	Can cause panic or CPA confusion	"What's driving this loss—depreciation or ops?"
No cost seg study	Missed year-1 tax shelter	"Will you perform a cost segregation study?"
REP misuse	IRS audit risk	"Do I qualify—and can we document it?"
Bonus depreciation assumed	Pro forma distortion	"How does this pencil without it?"

Red Flag	Why It Matters	What to Ask
No exit tax strategy	Surprise recapture bill	"How will LPs be impacted at exit?"

📌 Final Thoughts—The LP Tax Mindset

💬 Closing Analogy:

Imagine two investors both earn 15% returns. One pays 35% of that in taxes. The other pays nearly zero for the first 5 years—using depreciation, timing, and planning. Over a decade, the difference isn't marginal—it's generational.

Your job isn't to outsmart the IRS.
It's to **understand the rules well enough** to let them work for you.

🚩 Red Flags Recap—Chapter 20

1. **Misunderstanding Paper Losses**
   K-1 losses often mean tax savings—not bad performance.
2. **Assuming All CPAs Are Equal**
   Real estate investing demands a specialist CPA.
3. **Skipping Cost Seg Studies**
   If the deal qualifies and doesn't do one, you're leaving money behind.
4. **Blind Faith in Bonus Depreciation**
   Don't base decisions on legislation that might not pass.
5. **No Exit Tax Plan**
   Recapture and gains are real—plan ahead.
6. **Improper REP/STR Claims**
   These can be powerful or dangerous—use with precision.

CHAPTER 21
1031 EXCHANGES, SELF-DIRECTED IRAS & OPPORTUNITY ZONES

Avoiding the Red Flags of Capital Gains Taxes
What to Know Before You Sell—So You Don't Get Burned After

If you've ever sold an investment property and watched a chunk of your profit vanish to taxes, you're not alone.

Capital gains can take a **15%–20%** bite out of your return—plus **depreciation recapture at up to 25%**, and potentially state taxes on top.

But the best investors know:

You don't just build wealth by making more.
You build it by **keeping more**.

Three of the most powerful ways to keep more:

- 🔁 1031 Exchanges (for real estate)
- ▦ Opportunity Zones (for nearly any capital gain)
- 💼 Self-Directed IRAs (for tax-deferred or tax-free investing)

Each of these strategies can transform your after-tax return.
Each also comes with rules, deadlines, and traps.

Used correctly, they're the tools of the ultra-wealthy. Used carelessly? They're landmines.

What Is a 1031 Exchange?

A 1031 lets you **defer** capital gains tax by reinvesting proceeds from one investment property into another "like-kind" property. You must:

- Use a **qualified intermediary (QI)**
- Follow **strict timelines**
- Reinvest **into real estate only**

It's not tax-free—it's **tax-deferred**. You kick the can down the road. And in the right hands, that's a powerful wealth-building tool.

Why the Wealthy Love It

Imagine selling a $1 million property and rolling that into a $1.5 million deal, using leverage and avoiding a $300K tax hit.

Now imagine doing that **five times in 30 years**, never paying tax, and finally passing it to your heirs—who receive it at a **stepped-up basis**, wiping out the tax bill entirely.

That's not a loophole. It's the playbook.

▶ Red Flag: A 1031 Must Be Planned in Advance

You **can't do it retroactively**. If the sale closes and you've touched the funds—even accidentally—it's over.

You need:

- Written intent to exchange
- A qualified intermediary in place
- Sale proceeds held in escrow (you can't touch them)

- Title and taxpayer ID to match from sale to purchase

⚠ Once you've "cashed out," there's no going back.

Can LPs Use a 1031?

Short answer: **Not directly.**

Why? LP interests are **securities**, not real estate. They don't qualify for a 1031 under IRS rules.

But there's a workaround...

🧩 The "Drop and Swap" Strategy

Here's how it works:

1. **Drop:** Before a property is sold, the sponsor converts ownership into a **Tenant-in-Common (TIC)** structure. Each LP receives a direct, deeded interest.
2. **Swap:** You now own real estate directly—and can execute a 1031.

Sounds simple? It's not. It requires legal precision, pre-negotiation, and cooperation from the sponsor. Many won't offer it.

☑ Ask before investing:
"Do you allow for 1031-compatible exit structures like TIC or DST?"

☑ How to Execute a 1031 as an LP (If Offered)

Step	Requirement
1.	Confirm the deal offers TIC/DST exit options
2.	Hire a Qualified Intermediary (QI) **before** sale
3.	Identify up to 3 replacement properties in 45 days

Step	Requirement
4.	Close on a new deal within 180 days
5.	File Form 8824 with your CPA

These timelines are **not** suggestions—they're laws.

What Qualifies as "Like-Kind"?

More deals qualify than you might expect:

☑ **Allowed:**

- Residential → Commercial
- Apartments → Self-storage
- Office → Land
- Duplex → NNN lease property

✗ **Not allowed:**

- LP shares → LP shares
- Fund interests → REITs
- Real estate → Stocks, crypto, art

DSTs (Delaware Statutory Trusts) are structured to be 1031-compatible and passive—ideal for LPs who want hands-off investing.

▶ Common 1031 Mistakes That Blow Up a Deal

Mistake	Why It's Fatal
✗ Missed 45/180 Day Windows	IRS won't budge—even if you're 1 day late
✗ Touched the Funds	Even for 24 hours—deal is disqualified
✗ Took Partial Cash ("Boot")	That portion becomes taxable
✗ Wrong Name on Title	Must match selling entity's name
✗ No Qualified Intermediary	Deal fails without one

When a 1031 Makes (or Doesn't Make) Sense

☑ **Best Use Cases:**

- High-dollar capital gain
- You want to stay invested long term
- Sponsor supports 1031 exit options
- You want to avoid depreciation recapture now

✗ **Poor Fit:**

- You want liquidity
- You're near retirement
- You plan to reset your basis
- You're unsure of your next investment

🔄 Think of a 1031 as trading up—not cashing out.

Opportunity Zones: The 1031 Alternative for Any Asset Class

OZs were created in 2017 to spur investment in underserved areas. They offer:

1. **Deferral** of capital gains tax until 2026 (soon to expire)
2. **Elimination** of tax on **new gains** if held 10+ years

OZs Unlock for More Than Real Estate

Unlike 1031s, **any capital gain** qualifies:

- Stock sales
- Crypto gains
- Business exits
- Art sales
- Syndication exits

⚠ **Key Deadlines**

You must reinvest within **180 days** of the gain event. After 2026, the deferral benefit sunsets—but the **gain elimination** remains in place.

> ▶ **Red Flag: Not All OZ Funds Are Worth It**

Some funds market the tax benefit but underwrite terrible deals.

Ask:

- What's the **business plan**, not just the tax angle?
- How do you project returns **before tax benefits**?
- What's the **exit strategy** in 10+ years?
- Does this deal pencil without OZ status?

If a deal only looks good because of a tax break, it's probably not a good deal.

Quick Comparison Table: 1031 vs. Opportunity Zone

Feature	1031 Exchange	Opportunity Zone
Asset Type	Real estate only	Any capital gain
Timeline	45/180 days	180 days
Tax Deferral	☑	☑ (until 12/31/26)
Tax Elimination	✗	☑ (on new gain)
Passive Option	☑ (DST)	☑ (QOF)
Complexity	High	Moderate
Flexibility	Low	Medium
Ideal For	Real estate pros	Any long-term investor

Self-Directed IRAs (SDIRAs): Shield Growth from Uncle Sam

Self-Directed IRAs let you deploy retirement funds into alternative assets like:

- Real estate syndications
- Private equity
- Notes or hard money lending
- Precious metals

Why Investors Use SDIRAs

- Tax-deferred (Traditional) or tax-free growth (Roth)
- Escape market volatility
- Invest in what you know

Real-World Example

You invest $75,000 from your Roth SDIRA into a self-storage syndication.

In 6 years:

- The asset sells
- You receive $145,000
- **You owe $0 in taxes**

No capital gains. No income tax. Total return? Yours to keep.

⚠ UBIT: The Silent Killer of SDIRA Returns

UBIT = **Unrelated Business Income Tax**

Here's when it applies:

- Your SDIRA invests in a deal that uses **leverage**
- The debt-financed portion of your gains is **taxable** inside the IRA

- Often triggered by real estate syndications

💡 UBIT doesn't make the deal bad—it just reduces your after-tax return. Know before you go.

Common SDIRA Mistakes to Avoid

Mistake	Why It's Risky
✘ Assuming IRAs Are Tax-Free	Not true if UBIT is triggered
✘ Using Checkbook LLCs	Without legal review, you risk disqualification
✘ Forgetting Form 990-T	IRS penalty if you don't report taxable income
✘ Co-mingling Funds	Mixing personal and IRA funds = major penalty
✘ Working With Clueless Sponsors	Many don't understand SDIRA compliance rules

☑ Questions to Ask Before Using an SDIRA

- "Is this deal using leverage?"
- "Will UBIT apply to SDIRA investors?"
- "Have you worked with custodians before?"
- "Can your CPA and attorney support SDIRA compliance?"

If your sponsor gives you a blank stare—walk away.

Pro Tip: Combine SDIRAs With Roth Conversion

Want tax-free gains for life?

1. Convert Traditional IRA funds to a **Roth SDIRA**
2. Pay taxes on the conversion (ideally in a low-income year)
3. Invest in a high-growth syndication

Result: All future gains—**including distributions and sale proceeds**—are tax-free.

This is especially powerful for younger investors with long time horizons.

They reward the ones who started thinking **years before**.

🔨 The Capital Gains Tax Hit—Real Numbers

Case Study: The Silent Killer of Returns
Investor A sells a duplex bought for $500K, now worth $800K. After closing costs, net gain is $250K.

Without planning:

- Federal cap gains: 20%
- Depreciation recapture: 25%
- State tax (CA, NY, etc.): 8–13%

Total tax bill: $70,000–$90,000+
Without deferral or shielding, that's 30% of your equity **evaporated**.

Key Insight: A strong return doesn't matter if taxes drain it at the finish line.

🔨 1031s—Real-World Timeline Breakdown

The 1031 Process—LP Walkthrough

Day	Step
0	Close on property sale (must have QI set up)
1–45	Identify 1–3 potential replacement properties
46–180	Close on at least one property
181+	Submit Form 8824 with next tax return

🚩 **Common Misstep:** Identifying more than 3 properties without qualifying under the 200% or 95% rule = disqualification.

🏷️ 1031 Wealth-Building Example

The Snowball Strategy
Investor rolls gains from a $400K profit in Deal 1 into a $1.2M property (Deal 2). That gains another $400K and gets rolled again into a $2M asset (Deal 3).

After 3 cycles:

- No capital gains tax paid
- Paper wealth: $2M+
- Tax bill: still deferred
- Heirs receive stepped-up basis upon death = **tax wiped out**

🏷️ DSTs for LPs—What to Know

DSTs (Delaware Statutory Trusts):

- Pre-packaged, passive real estate investments
- 1031-eligible
- Popular among retiring investors
- Low control, low headache, moderate returns

☑ **When to Use a DST:**

- You want to complete a 1031 but don't want to be active
- You're facing a 180-day deadline and need a fallback
- You want income with minimal risk

⚠ **When NOT to Use One:**

- You want control over operations
- You're seeking high-upside/value-add deals

- You need liquidity (DSTs are highly illiquid)

📌 Opportunity Zones—Smart Uses & Traps

Investor Scenario:
You exit a startup with $500K in gains. Instead of paying taxes, you invest in an OZ fund developing affordable housing.

Benefits:

- Defer original gain until 2026
- After 10 years, all new appreciation = tax-free

▶ **Red Flag:** Fund relies *only* on the tax benefit to justify weak underwriting. Always ask:
Always ask, "Would I still invest in this if there were zero tax benefits?"

OZ Tip: They're most powerful when:

- You're investing early in a long-term project
- You believe in the **underlying asset**, not just the zone

📌 Extra Comparison Table—OZ vs 1031 for LPs

Feature	1031 Exchange	Opportunity Zone
Eligible Assets	Real estate only	Any capital gain
Tax Deferral	Yes	Yes (until 2026)
Tax Elimination	No	Yes (on new gains after 10 years)
Reinvestment Deadline	45/180 days	180 days
Passive Option	Yes (DST)	Yes (QOF)
Popular with	Active RE investors	Business owners, crypto holders
State Tax Impact	Deferred	May vary by state

Feature	1031 Exchange	Opportunity Zone
Best Use Case	Rolling RE equity	Non-RE gains with long horizon

🔨 SDIRAs—Mistakes LPs Make

▶ **Pitfall: Using Leverage Without Understanding UBIT**

Example:
Investor uses SDIRA to buy into a syndicated deal with 70% loan-to-value (LTV). Deal returns $50K on a $100K investment.

Roughly 70% of that gain ($35K) may be subject to UBIT if not planned for—and the IRS may charge 35%+ on that amount.

⚠ Many investors don't even know this happened until they get hit with a tax bill **and penalties**.

☑ **Ask Your Sponsor:**

"What portion of returns is tied to debt financing? Will your CPA assist in calculating UBIT exposure?"

🔨 SDIRA—Custodian Questions Checklist

Before using an SDIRA, ask your custodian:

- "Do you allow direct investments into LLC-based real estate syndications?"
- "Will you coordinate directly with my sponsor or attorney?"
- "Can you issue K-1s or Form 990-T support?"
- "How do you report UDFI (Unrelated Debt-Financed Income)?"

▶ **Mini Red Flag:** A sponsor says, "We've never worked with an SDIRA investor before." That's your cue to pause.

SDIRA Use Cases—When It Works Best

Best Scenarios for SDIRA Use:

- You're investing in **debt funds** (no leverage = no UBIT)
- You're buying a **long-term, stabilized deal**
- You plan to **leave the funds untouched until retirement**

Avoid If:

- You're in high-leverage syndications
- You need liquidity
- You want depreciation to offset your current taxes (IRAs can't use it personally)

Roth Conversion Timing Strategy

When to Convert to Roth:

- You're temporarily in a low-income year
- The market is down (convert at a lower valuation)
- Before investing in a high-growth, long-hold asset

▶ **Warning:** Roth conversions are **permanent**. Don't convert blindly—have your CPA model it out.

Bonus FAQs for Tax Shielding Strategies

Q: Can I 1031 into a fund?
A: Not usually. Most funds are partnerships. Only **DSTs** or **TICs** may qualify.

Q: Can I 1031 out of an Opportunity Zone investment?
A: No. OZs don't support 1031 exchange outflows. You must sell and pay taxes unless other strategies apply.

Q: Can I use an SDIRA to invest in a 1031-compatible deal?
A: You can invest in the real estate—but an SDIRA **can't do a 1031 exchange.** That's an individual-level tax deferral strategy.

Visual Summary—Which Tool to Use?

Decision Matrix: Which Tax Shield Fits Best?

Your Goal	Best Strategy
Defer RE gains	1031
Eliminate non-RE gains	OZ
Shield retirement funds	SDIRA
Passive, zero tax on growth	Roth SDIRA
Avoid recapture entirely	OZ + long hold
Simplify estate tax planning	1031 + stepped-up basis

Final Thought—Tax Shields as a Strategy, Not a Shortcut

Analogy to Close the Chapter:

Think of your capital as soldiers. Every tax you pay is a soldier lost in battle.
But tools like 1031s, OZs, and SDIRAs are the body armor that protects your army.

Used wisely, they help you **win the war over time—not just survive the next battle.**

▶ Red Flags Recap—Chapter 21: 1031s, SDIRAs & Opportunity Zones

1. **Planning a 1031 Too Late**
   No written intent? No QI? You're out of luck.
2. **Assuming LP Shares Qualify**
   You need TIC/DST to make a 1031 work as an LP.

3. **Letting Tax Benefits Justify Bad Deals**
   If it's a bad deal without the tax break, it's still a bad deal.
4. **Triggering UBIT Without Knowing It**
   Leverage + SDIRA = potential tax liability.
5. **Using Poorly Structured SDIRA Entities**
   One wrong move with a checkbook LLC can destroy your tax benefits.
6. **Failing to Ask Sponsors About Compliance**
   If they've never worked with SDIRA or OZ investors, that's your risk to carry.

Final Thought: Taxes Don't Have to Be Your Enemy

Capital gains taxes can erode decades of compounding.

But when you understand the tools available:

- **1031s** help you defer
- **OZs** can help you eliminate
- **SDIRAs** help you shield

The best time to plan? **Before the sale.**
Because the IRS doesn't reward people who think about taxes in April.

CHAPTER 22
TAX PITFALLS—WHAT CPAS WISH LPS KNEW

Tax Pitfalls—What CPAs Wish LPs Knew
The Mistakes That Cost You Thousands—And the Questions That Could Have Prevented Them

Most investors love the *idea* of real estate's tax advantages.
Far fewer understand how to actually *use* them.

And that's where things go sideways.

Your CPA might be excellent at filing a return.
But they can't optimize what they don't know. They don't know what syndications you're in. They don't know when your deals are exiting. And they don't have time in April to back into a strategy you never planned for.

What's worse: most tax mistakes don't feel like mistakes in the moment.
They only show up when the IRS does—or when your refund is half what you expected.

In this chapter, we'll unpack the most common tax traps passive investors fall into. These aren't rare technical errors. They're the predictable, avoidable blind spots that cost LPs tens (or hundreds) of thousands over time.

Avoiding them won't just protect your downside. It can *meaningfully* boost your upside—especially if you invest across multiple deals or intend to scale.

⚠ Pitfall #1: Forgetting About Depreciation Recapture

Depreciation is a gift... with strings attached.

Every year, you get to reduce your taxable income by writing down the value of the property—even if its actual market value is increasing. This paper loss can offset rental income and help you report "negative" income while still receiving real cash distributions.

But don't get too comfortable.
When the property sells, the IRS takes a closer look. And if you've taken significant depreciation (especially accelerated bonus depreciation), you'll owe a **recapture tax**, often at a flat 25%.

Investor Story: The Surprise Exit Bill

Amanda was thrilled when a multifamily deal returned $160K on her $100K investment.
Her CPA told her she owed tax on the $60K profit.
But then came the kicker: she also owed **recapture tax on $50K** in depreciation she had taken—an extra $12,500 she hadn't budgeted for.

☑ Solutions:

- **Ask for a recapture estimate** before a sale occurs.
- **Pair gains with losses**—harvest losses from stocks or other investments.
- **Use a 1031 exchange** to defer both capital gains and recapture (if allowed).
- **Mentally treat depreciation as a loan, not a rebate.** You'll eventually have to repay some or all of it unless your planning says otherwise.

⚠ Pitfall #2: Misapplying Passive Losses

One of the most misunderstood areas in real estate taxation is how *passive losses* work.

You may receive a K-1 showing a $30,000 loss and think, "Awesome—I get to deduct this from my W-2 income."

Not so fast.

Unless you (or your spouse) qualify as a **Real Estate Professional (REP)** or use the **Short-Term Rental (STR)** loophole, these losses are passive—and can only offset other passive income sources.

⚠ Common LP Mistake:

Treating K-1 losses like a tax refund.
In reality, they are suspended and stored until they can be matched against passive income or gains.

How Carryforwards Work:

- **Year 1:** $30K passive loss
- **Year 2:** No passive income → loss is suspended
- **Year 3:** $20K in passive gains → $20K offset, $10K rolls forward
- **Sale Year:** Remaining loss applies against gain → reduced taxes

☑ Solutions:

- **Track suspended losses** annually. Ask your CPA for a carryforward report.
- **Time your deals** so new passive income can use older passive losses.
- **Strategically leverage REP status** if one spouse can qualify.

- **Be cautious with expectations**—losses don't help until they're applied.

⚠ Pitfall #3: Missing or Mishandling K-1s

A K-1 is your annual report card for each syndication. It summarizes your share of:

- Income
- Losses
- Depreciation
- Capital gains
- Distributions
- Ownership interest

Miss one, and your return is wrong. Worse? The IRS already has a copy. And if you underreport income or gains, you risk audits and penalties.

Common Scenarios:

- You're in 7 deals. Only 5 K-1s arrive. You forget the rest.
- You assume your CPA has them. They don't.
- You file early... only to receive a late K-1 in April. Now you're amending.

☑ Solutions:

- **Create a centralized system**: Deal folders, K-1 checklist, sponsor contacts.
- **Email sponsors each February** asking when to expect K-1s.
- **Always file an extension** if a K-1 is delayed. It's normal in this space.
- **If investing via SDIRA**, remember that *state-level K-1s may be required too.*

⚠ Pitfall #4: Assuming All Syndications Offer Equal Tax Benefits

Every asset class behaves differently—and that includes how it treats taxes.

Some syndications are built to maximize depreciation. Others barely offer any. And some, like debt funds, offer zero shelter at all.

Asset Class	Depreciation?	Tax Treatment Notes
Multifamily	☑ High	Great for bonus depreciation
Self-Storage	☑ High	Strong early cash flow + cost seg
Retail	⚠ Medium	Variable depending on tenants
Raw Land	✘ None	No depreciation, limited sheltering
Development	⚠ Deferred	No depreciation until stabilization
Debt Funds	✘ None	Taxed as ordinary interest income

☑ Questions to Ask:

- "Will this deal include a **cost seg study**?"
- "When will depreciation begin?"
- "Is bonus depreciation still in play—or has it phased out?"

⚠ Pitfall #5: Hiring the Wrong CPA

A generalist CPA is fine for W-2 employees.

But once you enter the world of partnerships, depreciation, and passive loss limitations, you need a real estate tax specialist.

✘ Signs Your CPA Isn't the Right Fit:

- Doesn't understand K-1s
- Thinks passive losses apply to all income
- Never asks about basis or carryforwards
- Only contacts you in March or April

☑ **How to Vet a CPA:**

- "How many real estate syndication clients do you serve?"
- "How do you track basis and suspended losses?"
- "Can you help with 1031 exchanges or QOF strategies?"
- "Do you file multi-state K-1s?"

Good tax planning is proactive. Not reactive.
Your CPA should be an advisor—not just a form filler.

⚠ Pitfall #6: Not Tracking or Organizing Across Deals

As you add more syndications, tax complexity increases.
Missed K-1s, unclaimed losses, forgotten capital contributions, and exit recapture can quickly spiral.

And the IRS doesn't care how complicated your spreadsheet is. They expect your numbers to match theirs.

☑ **How to Systematize:**

- Use a **tax organizer** spreadsheet:
    - Deal name
    - Year invested
    - Sponsor
    - Distributions
    - Paper losses
    - Estimated recapture
    - Exit date
- Create a folder system by year and by deal:
    - /2024/OakwoodSelfStorage/K1.pdf
    - /2024/OakwoodSelfStorage/PPM.pdf

⚠ Pitfall #7: Misunderstanding SDIRA Tax Impact

Investing through a **Self-Directed IRA** (SDIRA) can be a great strategy—but it comes with hidden tax risks:

- **UBIT (Unrelated Business Income Tax)** may apply if the deal uses leverage.
- You may owe taxes via **Form 990-T**, even inside your IRA.
- Not all custodians understand how to handle these filings correctly.

☑ What to Know:

- Ask your sponsor if the deal uses leverage that could trigger UBIT.
- Confirm whether **UBTI shielding strategies** are being used.
- Make sure your custodian understands real estate—and can file Form 990-T.

▶ Red Flags Recap—Expanded Chapter 22

Here's a quick summary of the seven key tax traps covered—and the red flags you need to spot early:

1. **Forgetting About Depreciation Recapture**
   Those paper losses aren't "free money." They're deferred taxes—and the IRS collects when the deal exits.
2. **Misapplying Passive Losses**
   Passive losses offset passive income—not W-2 wages or active business earnings (unless you qualify under REP/STR rules).
3. **Late or Missing K-1s**
   If you don't track them, you'll misfile. If you file without them, you risk penalties. Always follow up—and file extensions when needed.

4. **Assuming All Asset Classes Are Equal**
   Some syndications (like land, development, or debt funds) offer little to no tax sheltering. Know what kind of depreciation you're getting.
5. **Working With a CPA Who Doesn't Specialize**
   A generalist may get your return filed—but can cost you six figures over time through missed opportunities and bad advice.
6. **Not Organizing or Tracking Across Deals**
   The more deals you're in, the more room for error. A missing K-1 or forgotten capital contribution can trigger costly consequences.
7. **Misunderstanding SDIRA Tax Impact**
   IRAs aren't always tax-free in leveraged deals. UBIT and Form 990-T can apply. You *must* understand the rules—or work with someone who does.

💬 Final Word: You Don't Need to Be a CPA—You Just Need a Playbook

The goal isn't perfection. It's awareness.
You don't need to memorize tax code. But you *do* need to ask better questions, surround yourself with pros, and keep your records sharp.

Because tax strategy isn't something you do in April.
It's something you build into every deal, every CPA conversation, and every investment decision—year-round.

Use the tax code. Don't fight it.
And don't leave six-figure value on the table because of things you "thought" your CPA was handling.

If you treat syndications like stocks or ignore what your K-1 is telling you, you're missing half the value of the investment.

The good news?

You don't have to be a tax expert.
You just need to ask better questions, avoid common mistakes, and surround yourself with pros who understand the rules of the game.

PART VII
THE BIGGER PICTURE

CONCLUSION
THE REASON WE DO IT ALL

Wealth Isn't Just About Money—It's About Meaning

Let's be clear:
This game we're playing—investing, protecting capital, building wealth—isn't about hoarding.
It's about *freedom*.
It's about *peace of mind*.
And more than anything, it's about showing up—for the people and causes we care about.

▶ The red flag no one talks about?
We chase wealth for the wrong reasons.
We think it's about the car, the house, the image.
We try to look successful before we actually are.
And in that chase, we trade what matters for what's visible:
Time for trinkets.
Joy for stress.
Generosity for status.

What Real Discipline Looks Like

Financial discipline doesn't mean being cheap.
It's not about skipping dinners or flying coach to prove a point.

True discipline is knowing *why* you're building.
It's choosing a home that fits your life—not your Instagram feed.
A car that gets you there—not one that puts you in debt.
A deal that aligns with your goals—not one that feeds your ego.

▶ **The biggest red flag?**
Living like someone you're not to impress people who don't matter.

What Wealth Really Buys

Most people think wealth is what they can *show*.
But real wealth is what you can *choose*.

It's:

- The ability to say no to the wrong deal
- The space to be there for your kids
- The margin to help a friend in crisis
- The calm of knowing your money is working—so you don't have to

That's why we do this.
Not for *more*.
But for *enough*.

Stop Chasing. Start Building.

We've all heard it:

"If you don't find a way to make money while you sleep, you'll work until you die."—Warren Buffett

But the part people miss?
You're not just building income streams.
You're building a life—with P*urpose*.
One that doesn't leave you drained or distracted.

And when you reach stability, remember why you started.

Why I Give

Wealth is a tool.
And the best use of any tool is to build something bigger than yourself.

Giving is how we stay grounded.
It's how we remember that this journey was never just about *accumulation*.
It was always about *impact*.

Not every return shows up on a spreadsheet.
Some of the best outcomes come from the deals you walk away from—and the unexpected moments along the way.

The Return You Don't Plan For

A few years ago, I walked away from a deal.
The numbers didn't make sense, so I passed.

But while walking the property, the seller mentioned a dog had wandered in.
No collar. No chip. Just a stray looking for a second chance.

We took him in temporarily. Posted signs. Waited.
No one claimed him.

We named him *Itty Bitty*.
And now, he's family.

Small. Scrappy. Fully in charge of the garage.

That dog wasn't part of the investment.
But he was the *unexpected return*.
A reminder that not all ROI is financial—and not all rewards are planned.

Full Circle

This book started with a simple idea:
Learn to recognize red flags so you can invest with confidence.
But the deeper truth is this:
Your story isn't just about numbers.
It's about discipline.
It's about alignment.
It's about backing yourself—without going it alone.

You start by learning.
Then you find the right partners.
And you keep asking better questions.

Because the real return isn't in the deal.
It's in the *freedom* to live the life you were meant to.

Want more resources or to be added to our email list scan the QR code below.

https://go.passive.investments/info

Having trouble with the QR code?
Feel free to email us directly at **carson@passive.investments**
(Note: There's no ".com"—".investments" is the full domain.)

NEXT UP
GLOSSARY & CALCULATIONS

Before you dive into your next deal—or walk away from one—you need more than intuition.

You need fluency.

This next section is your tactical toolkit:

- The definitions behind the buzzwords
- The formulas behind the returns
- And the red flags hidden in the fine print

Whether you're double-checking a waterfall, decoding a K-1, or just trying to speak the language with confidence—this chapter's your back pocket guide.

Let's break it down.

Glossary & Calculations: What Every Passive Investor Should Know and Use

Investing passively doesn't mean being uninformed.
The strongest LPs aren't just wiring capital—they're interpreting deal metrics, spotting sponsor assumptions, and knowing how to pressure-test a pro forma.

This expanded glossary goes beyond definitions. It includes:

- What each term means
- Why it matters
- How to calculate it

- What red flags to watch for
- Real-world examples
- Case studies, diagrams, and metric comparisons

Core Metrics

🟦 IRR (Internal Rate of Return)

Definition: The annualized rate of return factoring in the timing of cash flows.
Why It Matters: IRR reveals *how efficiently* capital is returned over time—not just how much.
Formula: Solved in Excel using =IRR(range of cash flows)

Example:

Year	Cash Flow
0	-$100,000
1	$5,000
2	$5,000
3	$5,000
4	$5,000
5	$130,000

IRR ≈ **15.2%**

Red Flags:

- ▶ IRR is high—but there's a massive capital event in Year 3 or 4 (unsustainable assumptions)
- ▶ No cash flow early on, all returns come from sale (you're gambling on the exit)

What to Ask:

- "How sensitive is this IRR to exit cap rate or refi timing?"
- "What percent of the IRR is from operating cash flow vs. sale proceeds?"

Cash-on-Cash Return (CoC)

Definition: Annual pre-tax cash flow / total cash invested
Why It Matters: Shows immediate income yield—crucial for income-focused investors

Formula:
Annual Cash Flow ÷ Equity Invested

Example:
If a deal distributes $8,000/year on a $100,000 investment:
CoC = **8%**

Real-World Benchmarks:

- ☑ Strong: 8–10%+ CoC (core-plus or value-add stabilized deals)
- ⚠ Moderate: 5–7%
- ▶ Weak: Under 5% without a compelling growth story

Red Flags:

- ▶ Sponsor touts high IRR but offers <3% CoC
- ▶ No distributions in the first 2–3 years ("We're reinvesting!"... or they're overleveraged)

Equity Multiple

Definition: Total cash returned ÷ total cash invested
Why It Matters: Tells you *how much* you got back, regardless of timing

THE RED FLAG PLAYBOOK

Formula:
(All Distributions + Exit Proceeds) ÷ Initial Investment

Example:
$100,000 invested → $220,000 returned over 6 years
Equity Multiple = **2.2x**

Red Flags:

- ▶ 2.0x multiple over 10 years (low yield, poor compounding)
- ▶ High multiple paired with low IRR = slow return of capital

What to Ask:

- "What's the hold period for this multiple?"
- "What % of that is from operations vs. exit?"

Investor Tip:
Compare IRR to equity multiple and hold period. High IRR with low equity multiple? Probably a fast-flip strategy. High multiple, low IRR? Probably a long hold with back-loaded returns.

🔁 Return Comparisons by Strategy

Strategy	IRR	CoC	Equity Multiple	Notes
Core	6–9%	4–6%	1.3–1.7x	Lower risk, stable cash flow
Core-Plus	8–12%	6–8%	1.6–2.0x	Slightly more upside, light value-add
Value-Add	13–18%	5–10%	1.8–2.5x	Rehab, rent increase, operating lift
Opportunistic	18%+	<5% (often)	2.5x+	High risk, heavy lift, backend returns
Development	20%+	None early	2.5–3.5x	Delayed returns, front-loaded risk

🏢 Cap Rate (Capitalization Rate)

Definition: A property's Net Operating Income (NOI) divided by its purchase price
Formula: Cap Rate = NOI ÷ Purchase Price
Why It Matters: Cap rate shows how much income a property produces *relative to its price*. It's a key metric for valuing deals and comparing risk.

Example:
NOI = $200,000
Purchase Price = $2,500,000
Cap Rate = 8.0%

Real-World Benchmarks:

Asset Type	Typical Cap Rate
Core Urban MF	3.5%–4.5%
Suburban MF	4.5%–6.0%
Self-Storage	5.5%–7.5%
Retail (Anchored)	6.0%–8.0%
RV Park / MH	7.0%–10.0%

Red Flags:

- ▶ Deal underwritten at a cap rate significantly *lower* than current comps
- ▶ Cap rate compression is required for return targets
- ▶ NOI inflated through unrealistic rent or occupancy assumptions

What to Ask:

- "What is the market cap rate today for similar properties?"
- "Is this an entry cap rate or a stabilized one?"

🚩 Preferred Return ("Pref")

Definition: The minimum return paid to LPs before the GP shares profits

Why It Matters: Prefs protect LPs by putting them first in the waterfall

Example:
A deal with an 8% pref:
LPs receive the first 8% annual return before the sponsor earns promote.

Red Flags:

- 🚩 Sponsor doesn't define the pref (or hides it deep in the docs)
- 🚩 No cumulative pref—missed payments aren't carried forward
- 🚩 Sponsor earns promote before LPs hit their pref
- 🚩 No catch-up or confusing waterfall language

FAQ Red Flags:
Q: "If the deal earns 7%, what happens?"
A: You get 7%, and the GP gets nothing—*if* the waterfall is structured correctly. If not, you may split even below the pref.

🎯 Promote / Waterfall Structure

Definition: The GP's share of profits after LPs receive a pref return

Why It Matters: Waterfalls control *how returns are split* as the deal performs.

Typical Structure:

1. **Pref to LPs** (e.g., 8%)
2. **Catch-Up** (optional—GP gets 100% until caught up with LPs)
3. **Split** (e.g., 70/30 LP/GP until IRR hurdle)
4. **Promote Tier** (e.g., 50/50 after 15% IRR)

Red Flags:

- ▶ Sponsor gets promote *before* returning full capital
- ▶ No cap on fees or promote tiers
- ▶ No catch-up clarity—ask: "Is it full or partial?"

What to Ask:

- "Is there a catch-up clause? Who gets what and when?"
- "Does the sponsor earn promote before full capital return?"

Waterfall Timing: When and How You Get Paid

A waterfall is the structure that governs how and when cash flows are split between LPs and GPs.

Below is a **typical waterfall with timing and thresholds**:

💧 Waterfall Example: $100,000 LP Investment

Step 1: Return of Capital
LP gets back the original $100,000 before any profit splits begin.

Step 2: Preferred Return (8%)
LP earns an 8% annual preferred return—**paid before the GP gets any promote**.
- If the deal generates $20K in profit per year, the first $8K goes to you annually until full pref is paid.

Step 3: GP Catch-Up (Optional)
Some waterfalls include a "catch-up" clause, where the GP gets **100% of profits** until they "catch up" to their share of the split (e.g., 30%).
- ▶ **Watch Out**: Catch-ups can eat into LP profits faster than you expect.

Step 4: Profit Splits (e.g., 70/30, then 60/40)
After preferred return and catch-up (if applicable), profits are split:

Tier	Threshold	LP Split	GP Split
Tier 1	Up to 15% IRR	70%	30%
Tier 2	Above 15% IRR	60%	40%

Step 5: Lookback Clause (Investor Protection)
If built in, this ensures the GP only keeps their promote **if the deal meets agreed performance**—and may return excess promote if it doesn't.

- ▶ **Missing Lookback**: Sponsors may walk away with a promote even if your returns disappoint.

Sponsor Fees & Waterfalls

Common Sponsor Fees

Fee Type	Typical Range	What It Covers
Acquisition Fee	1–3% of purchase price	Deal sourcing, due diligence
Asset Management	0.25–2% of revenue or value	Oversight of operations
Construction Management	5–10% of CapEx budget	Renovation oversight
Refinance Fee	0.5–2% of new loan	Incentive for recapitalization
Disposition Fee	1% of sale price	Sale execution
Promote (Carried Interest)	20–30%	GP's share of profits after LP pref

▶ **Red Flags:**

- Fees stacked without value creation.
- Promote earned before full capital return.
- No cap on cumulative fees.

🏢 Real-World Case Study: The "Fee Stack" That Crushed Returns

Deal: Value-add multifamily
Pro Forma: IRR = 16%, Equity Multiple = 1.9x
Actual Net to LPs: 1.4x after:

- 3% acquisition fee
- 2% annual asset management
- 1.5% refinance fee
- 1% disposition
- 30% promote

What Went Wrong:
Fees reduced net returns. Promote kicked in before full capital return.

Ask Next Time:

- "Is promote paid after full return of capital?"
- "Total fee load as % of deal?"
- "Is there a lookback or catch-up clause?"

📊 Visual: Return Flow for a Typical LP Investment

Capital In → Cash Flow → Return of Capital → Preferred Return → Profit Split

Example:

- $100K invested
- $8K/year cash flow
- 8% preferred return
- 70/30 split up to 15% IRR
- 60/40 thereafter

Watch For:

- Catch-up clauses that disproportionately reward GPs
- Missing lookbacks that ensure fairness over time

🔨 Final Tips for LPs

- **Don't just read returns—decode how they're paid.**
- **Scrutinize assumptions, timelines, and payout triggers.**
- **Ask for the full waterfall structure in writing—ideally with examples.**

📊 T12 (Trailing 12)

Definition: The last 12 months of actual property income & expenses
Why It Matters: The T12 tells you what's really happening—not just projections

Key Components:

- Rent roll
- Operating expenses
- Vacancy
- Management fees
- Repairs & maintenance

Red Flags:

- ▶ T12 not provided—only a pro forma
- ▶ Huge gap between T12 and projected Year 1 numbers
- ▶ Spikes or anomalies without explanation (e.g., sudden drop in expenses)

What to Ask:

- "How do your projections compare to the T12?"
- "What explains any major swings in the numbers?"

🏛 DSCR (Debt Service Coverage Ratio)

Definition: NOI ÷ Annual Debt Service
Why It Matters: DSCR measures the deal's ability to cover debt. Under 1.0 = trouble.

Formula:
DSCR = Net Operating Income ÷ Total Debt Payments

Example:
NOI = $150,000
Annual Debt = $100,000
DSCR = 1.5x

Benchmarks:

- ☑ Strong: 1.4x+
- ⚠ Average: 1.25x
- ▶ Weak: Below 1.15x

Red Flags:

- ▶ DSCR under 1.2x in base-case projection
- ▶ DSCR is inflated by unrealistic NOI growth
- ▶ Interest-only loan hides weak coverage in early years

What to Ask:

- "What's the DSCR year-by-year?"
- "How does it hold up in a stress test?"

📊 Pro Forma vs. Actuals

Definition:

- **Pro Forma:** Forward-looking projections
- **Actuals (T12):** Real historic data

Why It Matters: Many deals are sold on *pro forma dreams*, not financial reality.

Red Flags:

- ▶ Pro forma rents are 20%+ above current
- ▶ Expense reductions with no justification
- ▶ Sponsor markets "value-add" with zero historical upside data

What to Ask:

- "Show me the bridge from T12 to Year 1 pro forma"
- "What's been achieved so far on similar properties?"

ARR (Average Annual Return)

Definition: Average yearly return on investment.
Formula: (Total Profit ÷ Years Held) ÷ Initial Investment

Example:
$100K invested → $200K returned over 5 years → ARR = 20%

Why It Matters: Easy to explain, but ignores time value of money.

▶ **Red Flag:** Can overstate performance when used alone.
→ *Use it only as a cross-check against IRR.*

Legal & Structural Terms

- **Capital Account:** Tracks your contributions, income/loss, and distributions. Affects tax loss eligibility.
- **Subscription Agreement:** Binding contract between LP and sponsor.
- **Operating Agreement:** Governs the rules and profit splits. Read this carefully.
- **Indemnification Clause:** Defines GP legal protection—check for overreach.
- **Lookback Clause:** Ensures GPs don't keep promote if performance dips.
- **Catch-Up Clause:** GPs may get 100% of profits for a period after hitting pref—evaluate carefully.

Common Tax Terms

Term	Meaning	Why It Matters
Basis	Adjusted investment amount	Determines loss eligibility & tax due on sale
Suspended Losses	Unused losses due to passive activity rules	Carry forward until offset or disposition
UBIT/UBTI	Tax on leveraged IRA income	Applies to SDIRA investors
Recapture	Tax on depreciation at sale	Often taxed at 25%—plan ahead

K-1 Walkthrough: How to Read and Use It

Every LP receives a **Schedule K-1** each year for every partnership investment. It's the IRS form that shows your share of income, losses, deductions, and credits from the deal.

THE RED FLAG PLAYBOOK

Here's how to make sense of it:

📄 Key Boxes on the K-1

Box	What It Means	Why It Matters
Box 1	Ordinary Business Income/Loss	This affects your taxable income directly.
Box 2	Rental Real Estate Income/Loss	Most real estate deals report losses here due to depreciation.
Box 5	Interest Income	Taxable as ordinary income (e.g., from reserves).
Box 13	Deductions (e.g., depreciation, charitable)	Can reduce your tax bill—but subject to passive activity limits.
Box 16	Foreign Transactions	Rare, but must be reported if applicable.
Box 19	Distributions	What you were actually paid in cash. Doesn't always match taxable income.

▶ Red Flags to Watch

- **No K-1 by Tax Day**: Delayed filings can mess up your return and cause penalties.
- **Unexpected Box 1 Income**: Could indicate aggressive accounting or poor tax planning.
- **No depreciation in Box 13**: Is the sponsor even taking full advantage of tax benefits?

🔍 What to Do With It

- Give it to your CPA. They'll use it to complete your personal return.
- Track it annually—especially losses that carry forward if not used (suspended losses).
- Use it to calculate **basis** for when you exit the deal (determines taxable gain/loss).

GLOSSARY & CALCULATIONS

🔑 Key Glossary Terms

📃 Accredited Investor

Definition:
An individual or entity that meets specific income, net worth, or professional criteria established by the SEC to participate in certain private investment offerings.

Why It Matters:
Syndications often rely on exemptions under Regulation D (like Rule 506(b) or 506(c)) to avoid full SEC registration. These exemptions require investors to be accredited. Sponsors can't legally accept funds from non-accredited investors under certain structures. Knowing your status determines what deals you can access.

Who Qualifies:

- **Income Test:** $200,000 annual income ($300,000 with a spouse) in each of the last two years, with expectation of the same this year
- **Net Worth Test:** $1M+ net worth excluding primary residence
- **Professional Designation Test:** Certain licensed professionals (e.g., Series 7, 65, or 82 holders) qualify regardless of income or net worth
- **Entity Test:** Trusts or LLCs with $5M+ in assets, or where all owners are accredited

Red Flags:

⚑ Sponsor doesn't verify accreditation properly
⚑ You're asked to self-certify without a third-party letter for a 506(c) raise
⚑ The offering accepts non-accredited investors but doesn't offer the proper disclosures

Pro Tip:
If you're on the cusp of being accredited, talk to a CPA or financial advisor. You may be closer than you think based on asset structure or earned income. Some investors are accredited and don't realize it—especially if they include their spouse's income.

Depreciation

Definition:
A non-cash accounting deduction that spreads the cost of a property's physical assets over time—lowering taxable income.

Why It Matters:
Depreciation creates paper losses that can offset real income. This is one of the biggest tax benefits in real estate syndications.

Types:

- **Straight-Line Depreciation:** Residential = 27.5 years, Commercial = 39 years
- **Bonus Depreciation:** Allows you to write off 80–100% of qualifying assets in Year 1 (phasing down post-2022)
- **Cost Segregation:** Accelerates depreciation by breaking down components into 5-, 7-, 15-year schedules

Red Flags:
▶ Sponsor doesn't mention depreciation strategy in a tax-heavy deal
▶ No CPA or cost segregation firm involved
▶ Assumes 100% bonus depreciation in a year where it no longer applies

Example:
A $1,000,000 property might depreciate $36,363 annually on a straight-line basis (assuming commercial over 27.5 years). With bonus + cost seg, that number could jump to $250K+ in Year 1.

Investor Tip:
Check how depreciation is *allocated* to LPs on the K-1. Some sponsors take more than their share via special allocations.

Distributions

Definition:
Cash payouts sent to Limited Partners (LPs) based on income generated by the asset—typically monthly or quarterly.

Why It Matters:
Distributions are how you realize ongoing returns from an investment (vs. just waiting for the exit). But they also reveal how the asset is performing *right now*.

Types:

- **Preferred Return:** Minimum % to LPs before GP shares in profits
- **Return of Capital vs. Return on Capital:** Know whether you're getting back profits or just your own money.
- **Catch-Up Provisions:** Some GPs "catch up" on profits after preferred return is met

Red Flags:
▶ Distributions start immediately—even if the property isn't stabilized
▶ Inconsistent or skipped distributions without explanation
▶ No clear policy on waterfall triggers or cash reserves.

Example Timing:
A multifamily deal may target 8% preferred return with quarterly distributions of 2%. In Year 1, cash flow might be light due to renovations—but should stabilize over time.

Asset Class Tips:

- **Oil & Gas:** Often irregular and lumpy based on production

- **Multifamily:** More predictable once stabilized
- **Self-Storage:** Strong during economic downturns—can preserve distribution consistency

GP (General Partner)

Definition:
The active sponsor/operator of the deal. Responsible for acquisition, financing, asset management, investor relations, and executing the business plan.

Why It Matters:
Your money is tied to their judgment, ethics, and execution. A great GP can fix a bad deal. A bad GP can ruin a great one.

What They Do:

- Find the deal
- Secure financing
- Manage property or operations
- Communicate with investors
- Handle tax filings (K-1s)

Red Flags:
▶ No track record or experience in that asset class
▶ Overpromising and under-delivering on prior deals
▶ No skin in the game (i.e., no co-investment)

Sponsor Due Diligence Tip:
Ask what happens if something goes wrong. Do they personally guarantee debt? Do they use third-party property managers? Who's really in charge?

Asset Class

Definition:
A category of investment characterized by similar risk/return profiles and operational models (e.g., multifamily, self-storage, oil & gas, industrial).

Why It Matters:
Every asset class carries its own timeline, tenant base, risk profile, tax treatment, and operational red flags.

Examples:

- **Multifamily** – stable, high demand, lower volatility
- **Retail** – sensitive to e-commerce trends
- **Oil & Gas** – high tax benefits, high risk
- **Industrial** – distribution-focused, long leases
- **RV Parks** – fragmented but high cash flow potential

Bonus Depreciation

Definition:
A tax incentive allowing investors to deduct a large portion of an asset's cost in Year 1 (phased from 100% in 2022 down to 60% by 2025).

Why It Matters:
Creates massive paper losses early in the deal—offsetting other passive income.

Red Flags:

▶ Sponsor assumes 100% bonus depreciation without checking current IRS phase-out schedule
▶ No CPA or cost seg strategy discussed

CF (Crowdfunding)

Definition:
A method of investing in syndications through online platforms that pool small amounts from many investors.

Why It Matters:
Gives smaller investors access to private deals, but with trade-offs:

- Longer communication cycles
- Less transparency
- No direct relationship with GP

Red Flags:
▶ Sponsor hides behind the platform—no personal access
▶ Delayed K-1s or updates

Due Diligence

Definition:
The process of evaluating a sponsor, deal, and market before investing.

Why It Matters:
It's how you avoid capital loss. Passive doesn't mean blind.

Checklist Includes:

- Reviewing the sponsor's track record
- Scrutinizing the pro forma assumptions
- Understanding fee structures
- Asking "what if" stress test questions

Red Flags:
▶ Vague or missing underwriting assumptions
▶ Sponsor discourages or deflects detailed questions

Founder

Definition:
The originator of a deal or firm—often interchangeable with "sponsor" or "GP" but sometimes distinct.

Why It Matters:
Founders shape company culture, risk tolerance, and deal direction.

Investor Tip:
If the founder isn't involved in day-to-day asset management, ask who is.

LP (Limited Partner)

Definition:
A passive investor in a deal with limited liability and no control over operations.

Why It Matters:
You earn returns based on the GP's execution. You're protected legally from direct liability—but not from poor management.

Red Flags:
▶ Sponsor shifts too much risk to LPs
▶ LP capital used for GP fees early on

Private Placement Memorandum (PPM)

Definition:
The legal disclosure document outlining investment risks, sponsor structure, offering details, and disclaimers.

Why It Matters:
This is the fine print that governs your investment. It protects the sponsor legally—and outlines how your capital is used.

What to Look For:

- Clear description of business plan
- Waterfall structure
- Sponsor fees
- Risk factors

Red Flags:
▶ PPM delivered late or incomplete
▶ Doesn't match what was pitched

Pro Forma

Definition:
Forward-looking financial projections used to model a deal's future income, expenses, and returns.

Why It Matters:
Every projection is built on assumptions. Pro formas are not reality—they're a test of how realistic the sponsor's thinking is.

Red Flags:
▶ Rent growth projections with no comp support
▶ Cap rate compression without justification
▶ Low reserves or contingency planning

Cost Segregation Study (Cost Seg)

Definition:
A tax strategy that accelerates depreciation by breaking a property into components (like HVAC, flooring, or lighting) that can be depreciated over shorter time periods than the standard 27.5 or 39 years.

Why It Matters:
It can create large paper losses early in a deal—reducing taxable income and increasing after-tax returns.

Calculation: Requires a third-party engineering-based analysis to reclassify assets for faster depreciation (e.g., 5, 7, or 15-year schedules).

Red Flags:
▶ No study offered in deals with significant improvement budgets.
▶ Sponsors claiming huge write-offs without a proper study.

Real-World Tip: Ask when the study will be done and how the cost is being split between GP and LPs.

Risk-Adjusted Return

Definition:
The return of an investment relative to the level of risk taken. A high return doesn't mean much if the risk was unsustainably high.

Why It Matters:
Two deals with the same IRR could carry drastically different risk profiles.

Common Ratios:

- **Sharpe Ratio** (for stocks)
- **IRR vs. Equity Multiple vs. Hold Time** (for real estate)

Investor Tip:
Ask: "What assumptions must come true for this return to happen?"

Sponsor

Same as GP, but worth clarifying as a standalone term for beginner LPs.

Definition:
The person or team running the deal—responsible for finding, acquiring, managing, and exiting the asset.

Why It Matters:
You are investing in the sponsor first, property second. Execution is everything.

Syndication

Definition:
A pooled investment where multiple LPs contribute capital to a deal led by a GP or sponsor.

Why It Matters:
Allows LPs to access deals they couldn't fund solo—and brings scale and diversification to private investing.

Structure:

- LLC or LP formed
- GP runs the deal
- LPs contribute equity
- Profits split per the waterfall

Underwriting

Definition:
The financial modeling process used to evaluate a deal's potential performance, including rents, expenses, exit strategy, and more.

Why It Matters:
Flawed underwriting leads to flawed projections. This is where most bad deals begin.

Red Flags:
▶ Rent bumps without market comps
▶ Interest-only debt without refinance plan
▶ Low reserves or light expense assumptions

506(b)

Definition:
An SEC exemption allowing sponsors to raise capital privately from up to 35 non-accredited investors (plus unlimited accredited), but *no general solicitation* (i.e., advertising).

Red Flags:
▶ Sponsor promotes deal publicly on social media—violates SEC rules
▶ No documented "pre-existing relationship"

506(c)

Definition:
Another SEC exemption allowing *public* advertising—but **only** accredited investors can invest, and accreditation must be verified.

Red Flags:
▶ No accreditation verification performed
▶ Sponsor accepts non-accredited investors into a 506(c) deal

Blind Pool

Definition:
A fund where investors commit capital without knowing which specific assets will be acquired.

Red Flags:
▶ Used by inexperienced GPs who lack a real pipeline but want to raise capital anyway

Capital Stack

Definition:
The hierarchy of capital sources used to fund a deal—typically includes common equity, preferred equity, mezzanine debt, and senior debt.

Red Flags:
▶ Sponsors hiding your true position in the stack
▶ Creative language that makes common equity sound like preferred equity

Clawback Provision

Definition:
A clause that allows LPs to recover excess profits paid to the GP if return hurdles aren't met by the end of the project.

Red Flags:
▶ No clawback language in deals with aggressive waterfall structures
▶ Sponsor keeps all promote even if final returns miss projections

Break-Even Occupancy

Definition:
The occupancy rate a property needs to cover operating expenses and debt payments.

Red Flags:
▶ Break-even levels above 85%
▶ No buffer for economic vacancy or unexpected costs

KPI (Key Performance Indicator)

Definition:
A measurable value that shows how effectively a property or operator is meeting objectives like occupancy, NOI, and rent collection.

Red Flags:
▶ Sponsor fails to report KPIs post-close
▶ KPIs shared are cherry-picked and lack context

Lease-Up Risk

Definition:
The risk that a new development or repositioned asset takes longer than expected to reach stabilized occupancy.

Red Flags:
▶ Unrealistically fast lease-up timelines
▶ No marketing budget or proven team to execute the lease-up

Disposition Fee

Definition:
A fee paid to the sponsor upon the sale of the property.

Red Flags:
▶ Fee is paid regardless of performance
▶ Disposition fee exceeds 2% with no justification

Reversion Cap Rate

Definition:
The cap rate used to estimate a property's future sale value.

Red Flags:
▶ Exit cap rate is lower than the entry cap in today's market
▶ No stress testing on reversion assumptions in pro forma

🔖 Red Flag Metric Decoder

Metric	Common Misuse	What to Ask
IRR	Inflated by early exits or refis	"Is this based on model or actual payouts?"
Equity Multiple	Presented without timeframe	"What's the hold period?"
CoC Return	Gross numbers shown	"Net of expenses and reserves?"
ARR	Flat distributions assumed	"When are returns expected?"

🗣 FAQ: Real Questions from Real LPs

(What Most People Don't Ask—But Should)

This is your no-spin zone. These are the questions LPs actually worry about—the ones that pop up late at night after the webinar ends, before the wire is sent, or after the sponsor stops replying. We've heard them all. Here are the most important, answered without fluff.

❓ Can I invest in a deal if I'm not accredited?

Yes—sometimes. But it depends on the structure of the offering.

There are two common exemptions used under SEC Regulation D:

- **506(b)**: Allows up to 35 **non-accredited but sophisticated** investors. You must have a pre-existing, substantive relationship with the sponsor, and the deal **cannot be publicly advertised**. You must be financially literate enough to evaluate private securities risk.
- **506(c)**: Requires all investors to be **accredited**. These deals **can** be advertised, but sponsors are required to **verify** your income or net worth (W-2s, tax returns, CPA letter).

▶ **Red Flags:**

- Sponsor publicly markets a 506(b) deal.
- You're told, "Just check the accredited box and we're good."
- Sponsor skips the verification process entirely.

Pro Tip: If you're not accredited yet, build relationships. Ask good questions. Learn the process now so when you are accredited, you'll invest like a pro—not a beginner with capital.

? How do I know when I'm truly ready to invest?

You're ready when:

1. You can **articulate the deal** in plain English.
2. You've reviewed the **PPM, operating agreement, and underwriting** (not just the pitch deck).
3. You understand **how and when you get paid**—and what could go wrong.
4. You're investing from **a calm place**, not fear of missing out.

Most LP regrets come from skipping #3 and #4. Clarity, not charisma, should guide your decision.

▶ **Red Flags:**

- The deal sounds too good—but you don't fully understand how.
- You feel "late to the party."
- You're excited, but not clear.

? What's the typical timeline of a syndication investment?

Here's a simplified timeline:

1. **Due Diligence (2–3 weeks):** You review the deal, ask questions, attend webinars.

2. **Capital Raise (1–4 weeks):** Once the offering is live, you commit funds.
3. **Funding & Close (1–3 weeks):** You wire your capital.
4. **Stabilization (6–24 months):** The property is improved, leased, or repositioned.
5. **Cash Flow (varies):** Distributions begin—sometimes right away, sometimes after stabilization.
6. **Exit (3–7 years):** The property is sold or refinanced, and you (hopefully) receive a return of capital and profits.

▶ **Red Flags:**

- No clear timeline is communicated.
- Sponsor glosses over stabilization period risks.
- "Cash flow Day 1" promises in a heavy value-add deal.

? What if I want to exit early?

Short answer: Syndications are illiquid. But there may be options.

Some sponsors:

- Offer **buyback programs** (you may sell your interest at a discount).
- Facilitate **secondary transfers** (placing your interest with another investor).
- Allow **partial exits** during recapitalization events.

But these aren't guaranteed. Always check the PPM and operating agreement.

▶ **Red Flags:**

- Sponsor says, "You can sell anytime," with no paperwork to back it up.
- No secondary market or exit terms defined.

Pro Tip: Only invest capital you can afford to lock up. Liquidity is a premium feature—and syndications usually don't offer it.

? What happens if I make a mistake?

Let's break it down by scenario:

You picked a bad sponsor:

- Document everything. Share what you learned with peers. Pull back and analyze what you missed—was it the track record, the tone, the transparency?
- You may lose money. But if you learn the pattern, you'll save far more in the long run.

You didn't understand the waterfall:

- Ask questions now. It's better to clarify late than never. If the GP takes a huge promote and there's no preferred return, you may be last in line for profits.

You misfiled your taxes:

- Hire a CPA with syndication experience. Amend your return. Fix it fast. These issues are solvable—until you ignore them.

You overcommitted funds:

- Some LPs stretch into a deal and regret the illiquidity. Learn to leave cash on the sidelines for emergencies or new opportunities.

▶ **Red Flag:** Telling yourself, "It'll work out," without taking corrective action.

Bottom Line: Every investor has scar tissue. The difference is whether you compound the mistake—or grow from it.

? What if the sponsor disappears after I wire money?

This is every LP's nightmare. Here's what to do:

1. **Try multiple contact methods** (email, phone, investor portal).
2. **Reach out to other LPs** in the deal.
3. **Check your documents**: What rights do LPs have in this scenario?
4. **Request transparency in writing**—quarterly financials, updates, or a meeting.
5. **Escalate if needed**: A group of LPs may be able to initiate a vote or legal action.

▶ Red Flags:

- Sponsor replies to social media but not investors.
- Updates stop or get vague after funding closes.
- No financials, no K-1, no accountability.

Pro Tip: Silence is not a communication strategy. Good sponsors *over*-communicate when deals go sideways.

? Should I invest with friends or family?

Be very careful.

Pros:

- You know the person. There's trust.

Cons:

- Lack of professionalism: friends may not follow formal reporting or due diligence processes.
- If the deal goes south, **your relationship might, too**.

Ask:

- Is this friend a licensed sponsor or using a professional team?
- Will I receive a PPM, operating agreement, and regular updates?
- Would I invest in this deal if I didn't know them?

▶ **Red Flags:**

- "Trust me, it's going to be great."
- No formal documentation.
- You feel guilted into participating.

? How much should I invest in my first deal?

Only what you can afford to lose **without emotional fallout**.

Many new LPs go too big, too fast. Start with a test deal:

- $25K–$50K is common.
- Observe: How is reporting? Are they hitting milestones?
- Learn without risking too much.

▶ **Red Flags:**

- Sponsor has a $100K minimum, and you're nervous—but wiring anyway.
- You feel pressured because "everyone else is in."

? What should I expect in a quarterly report?

At a minimum:

- Rent collections / occupancy
- Progress on business plan (renovations, leasing, capex)
- Distributions (past, current, upcoming)
- Commentary on market trends or challenges

Red Flags:

- Boilerplate updates ("we are working hard" with no data)
- Long gaps between reports
- No explanation for missed distributions

Ask This, Not That:

- ☑ "Can you walk me through the last quarter's numbers?"
- ✗ "Is the deal doing okay?"

? What are typical fees in a syndication?

Fees vary, but common ones include:

- **Acquisition Fee:** 1%–3% of purchase price
- **Asset Management Fee:** 1%–2% of revenue or assets under management
- **Refinance/Disposition Fee:** 1%-2%
- **Promote (Carried Interest):** 20%-30% of profits after preferred return

▶ **Red Flags:**

- Fees not disclosed up front
- GP gets paid heavily before LPs see a return
- Promote structure favors GP even in mediocre performance

Pro Tip: Good sponsors make money **with you**, not **before you**.

? What's a preferred return—and should I expect one?

A preferred return (or "pref") means LPs get first dibs on profits—typically 6–10%—before GPs take a share.

Without a pref: GP and LP may split profits evenly from dollar one, which increases LP risk.

▶ **Red Flags:**

- No pref and high promote.
- GP gets 50% of profit despite underperformance.
- The "catch-up" clause eats into LP returns unnoticed.

? Should I reinvest distributions or wait for exits?

Depends on your goals.

- If you're cash flow focused, take the distributions and redeploy elsewhere.
- If you're building long-term wealth, reinvesting can boost compounding—but watch liquidity.

Some sponsors offer "auto-reinvest" programs. Read the fine print.

▶ **Red Flags:**

- Sponsor pushes reinvestment without giving performance options.
- No transparency on when capital is truly returned.

? Can I invest through my LLC or trust?

Yes, and often you should.

Benefits:

- Liability protection
- Estate planning
- Easier tracking for tax and legal purposes

BUT: Make sure your LLC is properly structured, funded, and documented.

▶ **Red Flags:**

- Sponsor won't accept entity investments.
- You don't have a clear operating agreement in place.

? Should I join an investor group or LP mastermind?

Yes—if:

- It's vetted and offers real value (deal reviews, red flag stories, expert access)
- The members are experienced or ask strong questions
- The group isn't just hype or cheerleading

LP masterminds can help you learn faster **and avoid sponsor marketing echo chambers.**

▶ **Red Flags:**

- Group is run by a sponsor pushing their own deals
- Everyone's "bullish" and no one talks risk

? What should I ask before wiring funds?

1. Have I read the full PPM and operating agreement?
2. Do I understand the capital stack, fees, and waterfall?
3. What happens if the deal underperforms—or fails?
4. What's the tax treatment? Will I receive a K-1? When?
5. Have I validated the sponsor's track record independently?

❓ FAQ Red Flags: Common Confusion Points

Q: Is a higher IRR always better?
▶ Not necessarily. High IRR can come from *early exits* or risky assumptions. IRR should align with the hold period, cash flow, and risk profile.

Q: Should I chase a high equity multiple?
Only if you're okay with long hold times and limited interim cash flow. A 2.5x over 10 years may *look* better than 2.0x over 5—but your money works slower.

Q: What's a good CoC if I'm investing for income?
Look for 7–10%+ CoC in stabilized or cash-flowing assets. Development deals often produce $0 for 2–3 years.

Q: What if the sponsor won't show their return breakdown?
▶ Major red flag. Sponsors should provide sensitivity tables showing returns under different exit caps, delays, or refi scenarios.

Q: Can I just use IRR to compare deals?
Only in part. You need *context*. A deal with 18% IRR and 2.0x equity multiple over 5 years is very different from one with 18% IRR and 1.6x over 3 years. The timing, risk, and yield profile all matter.

🎯 Ask This, Not That: Sponsor Question Edition

1. About Skin in the Game

✗ Don't Ask:
"How much of your own money is in the deal?"

☑ Ask Instead:
"How are our interests aligned—and how is your compensation structured across the life of the deal?"

Why: Even if they put money in, a sponsor can still extract more via fees. You're looking for alignment, not just a check.

2. About Returns

✗ Don't Ask:
"What's the projected IRR?"

☑ Ask Instead:
"What assumptions are driving that IRR—and when is most of the return expected?"

Why: A high IRR front-loaded with aggressive refinance assumptions is riskier than a lower one backed by solid cash flow.

3. About Experience

✗ Don't Ask:
"How many deals have you done?"

☑ Ask Instead:
"How many of your past deals hit pro forma—or missed it—and what did you learn from those?"
Why: It's not about deal count. It's about how they perform when things go sideways.

4. About the Business Plan

✗ Don't Ask:
"What's your renovation or value-add plan?"

☑ Ask Instead:
"What's the CapEx budget—and how confident are you in the contractor's ability to hit those numbers and timelines?"
Why: Execution risk is real. Anyone can write a plan. Few deliver it on time and under budget.

5. About Fees

✗ Don't Ask:
"What's your fee structure?"

☑ Ask Instead:
"What's the total fee load as a percentage of equity—and when does the promote kick in?"
Why: Fees add up fast. The real question is when the sponsor starts getting paid more than the LPs.

6. About Downside Protection

✗ Don't Ask:
"What happens if things don't go as planned?"

☑ Ask Instead:
"What's your backup strategy if occupancy drops, interest rates spike, or the exit gets delayed?"
Why: You're testing adaptability—not just optimism.

7. About Transparency

✗ Don't Ask:
"How often will I get updates?"

☑ Ask Instead:
"Can you show me a sample investor report from a current deal?"
Why: Anyone can say they communicate. You want proof of quality and cadence.

8. About Legal Protections

✗ Don't Ask:
"Is this SEC compliant?"

☑ **Ask Instead:**
"Which exemption are you filing under (506(b) or 506(c)), and can I review the PPM and Operating Agreement?"
Why: True compliance means legal clarity and document access—not vague reassurances.

9. About Exit Strategy

✗ **Don't Ask:**
"When do you plan to sell?"

☑ **Ask Instead:**
"What exit strategies are modeled, and how flexible is the plan if market conditions shift?"
Why: Fixed timelines are fragile. You want contingency thinking.

Final Word: Your Power Lives in the Questions You Ask

The best LPs aren't necessarily the wealthiest. They're the most prepared. The most skeptical. The most curious.

Every wire you send is a vote of confidence—not just in the deal, but in yourself. Ask better questions. Know your red flags. And remember:

Passive investing doesn't mean passive thinking.

Made in United States
Cleveland, OH
11 August 2025